Mouthful of Feathers
Upland in America

Mouthful of Feathers: Upland in America

Copyright © 2023 Reid Bryant, Ryan Busse, Edgar Castillo, Chris Dombrowski, Marissa Jensen, Michael Keaton, Chad Love, Jillian Lukiwski, Greg McReynolds, Michael Neiduski, T. Edward Nickens, Blaine Peetso, Christine Peterson, Thomas Reed, Bruce Smithhammer, Shauna Stephenson, Eric Thompson, Els Van Woert, Ben O. Williams, and David Zoby.

All rights reserved. No part of this book may be reproduced, stored, or transmitted in any form or by any means without the prior permission of the publisher, except for brief excerpts for reviews.

To request permissions, contact the publisher at editor@cornmillpress.com

Hardcover: ISBN 978-1-7333422-4-7

Paperback: ISBN 978-1-7333422-5-4

First hardcover edition July, 2023

Edited by Reid Bryant, Greg McReynolds and Thomas Reed

Cover art by Frederick Stivers

Cover and Interior Design by James Daley

Printed in the United States of America

Cornmill Press

16420 SE 31st Street

Bellevue, WA 98008

1-509-828-3300

cornmillpress.com

Table of Contents

Intro – The View From Here – The Editors 6
Foreword – Michael Keaton 8
Belief – Blaine Peetso 10
The Words We Use – Bruce Smithhammer 12
We Only Get So Many Octobers – Greg McReynolds 16
Liberty – Thomas Reed 20
Seven Times Slower – Jillian Lukiwski 24
Born of a Barstool – Ryan Busse 32
The Old Man's Gun – Thomas Reed 38
Won't You be My Neighbor – Edgar Castillo 54
Solitude – Greg McReynolds 62
Making Sense – T. Edward Nickens 68
What's Left of Lolo – Shauna Stephenson 74
Christmas Eve – Chris Dombrowski 84
Connection – Els Van Woert 94
On Love and Bird Dogs – Mike Neiduski 110
Autumn's Eve – Reid Bryant 118
Steady Yeti – The beauty of second chances – Marissa Jensen 126
The Best is Still to Come – Eric Thompson 132
Grouse Magic – David Zoby 140
A Lesson From the Bird Dog Who Turned Me Into a Hunter – Christine Peterson 150
Absolution in Four Acts – Chad Love 156
Gestures of Intent – Reid Bryant 164
Time Collection – Greg McReynolds 168
The Last Chicken – Thomas Reed 174
Parting Thoughts – A Life in the Uplands – Ben O Williams 182
Afterword – Bruce Smithhammer 186

Introduction
The View From Here

Optimism is embodied in the uplands. Our dogs know this better than we do. Upland hunting is searching for something we don't know is there, and the understanding that we may come up empty. A pup is the belief that we can do better, for the dog and for ourselves. In an era that somehow seems preoccupied with gloom, there are few anchors more genuine than a dog and few mediums more hopeful and optimistic than a dog turned loose into the uplands.

Some years ago, a couple of hunters who fancied themselves writers with a taste for good dogs and an occasional good joke, took a step into the (then) untracked blogosphere and started a website called Mouthful of Feathers. The idea was simple: we would write what we wanted and put it up for any and all to read, as long as it was good, as long as it had a connection, even a thin one, to the uplands. It was okay to say whatever needed saying, and it was okay to be irreverent, real, unvarnished.

Our words were sometimes heavy, sometimes light, and often, if not always, shared in the spirit of noticing the things that keep humans human. Whether tender, comedic or self-deprecating, we were always genuine.

Mouthful of Feathers has been many people and many things: a blog, an eBook, and a place to publish thoughts that don't fit inside the confines of the current outdoor press. It is also a mindset focused on wild birds, wild places and cherished dogs. Mostly, Mouthful of Feathers is a belief that words are enduring, that beauty is not fleeting, but tenacious. We know that good clings to the world and to us, even when we try to brush it away. Wild birds, wild places and dogs are beautiful; so are experiences, laughter, good guns, friends and family. It's actually all quite simple.

The writers of this book are spread across the country. They are authors new and old. Their backgrounds are different, and their worldviews are disparate.

Each of them understands the wonder of a wild bird, the allure of a secret place and the love of a dog. This is a place where we put aside differences and walk on common ground, sharing common joy. This is a place for uplanders, dog-lovers and fans of a well-crafted sentence. The only right and left in this book is the right side of the canyon or the left side of the wheatfield. Conservative is what you are when you are low on shells and a mile from the truck; liberal describes your pour from the bourbon bottle at the end of the day. Here, we set aside sides and we hunt, brag on our bird dogs, celebrate stories, and hopefully, enjoy.

Greg McReynolds, Pocatello, Idaho
Reid Bryant, Dorset, Vermont
Thomas Reed, Pony, Montana

Foreword
Michael Keaton

More than once have I turned my truck around and pulled back into my driveway, opened the back door and hoisted him off of my back seat. All 85 lbs and (now) 12 years of him. After pushing his wet muddy body off my coat, vest, shell bag, lunch etc, I have taken a lap or two around the truck just to loosen up my back, passing my crated setters now literally shaking with excitement and anticipation, and we haven't even left the driveway.

You'd think I would have developed the discipline to not look in the rear view mirror and see him sit back there with his graying face, watching me go with a look of absolute disbelief and melancholy as he got smaller and smaller in the rear view mirror.

An hour-plus, hot-coffee-spilling drive ahead of me and I wanted to get there before the conditions changed. At that moment, they were perfect. Good moisture on the ground and just enough of a light, dead-leaf-smelling breeze in the air to lift a nose and pick up a small tight covey one hundred yards away.

Rolling down a two-lane, I carried teammates. They were amped from the second they heard my boots, jacket, and thermos land on my bench in the mud room, predawn.

I'm someone who played organized sports most all of my life, and it wasn't until I made enough money to afford a good bird dog that I got to enjoy and actually cherish the experience of having an animal as my teammate. There were years of riding cutting horses and, trust me, having your teammate be a thousand pound animal under your butt and between your legs—amped up like a formula one race car—is a whole other deal.

But watching your teammate quarter back and forth across a dew-dampened field in early morning light, looking like a natural, graceful athlete, is such an extraordinary thing that I've literally heard myself say out loud, with no one else there, "God, I wish I could do that."

How many times have you apologized to your dog after missing an easy shot? Watching your partner come out of a thicket—after disappearing for fifteen minutes—holding a limp rooster in his mouth that you were sure was a lost cause will make your face hurt from smiling so hard.

In a little more than an hour, I'd be out of the truck. After one more sip of lukewarm coffee, I'd be putting collars on with cold hands and sliding shells into my scratched-up old side-by-side. I'd be in that coulee where, a couple of Octobers ago, I put up a covey. Maybe we'll get some shooting. Then again, maybe we won't. Maybe the dogs will do what they love to do and I'll just watch. After all, they know a hell of a lot more about it than I do.

"Hup!"

This book holds a collection of stories, essays, lies about, and meditations on the sport of bird hunting by women and men who have their own cherished experiences and insights. Far more than I, most likely.

Blaine Peetso
Belief

I believe in the magic of bird dogs,
black coffee on cold mornings,
overgrown two-track and caragana hedges,
abandoned homesteads, big Alberta skies,
the weathered wood of long forgotten corrals,
chokecherry thickets in the short grass hills
a sharptail's chuckle and rosehip jelly,
the coulee's edge where the grain gives way,
"the wild and thin wicked prairie wind",
numb cheeks, laugh lines, and crow's feet,
cracked windshields and Fred Eaglesmith,
"broke in" boots and beat-up shotguns,
beer on the tailgate, rye 'round the fire,
muskeg moss and birch bark, spruce stands,
golden aspen groves and the flush of The King,
Keen's hot mustard and coarse liver sausage
on a humble saltine, cutlines and cutblocks,
dusty logging roads neutered by hard frost,
the disappearance of a distant bell,
the chatter of fallen leaves underfoot,
and the smell of highbush cranberries,
in the way that the light just lingers
as the sun slants and summer dims.

I believe that I'll believe in this forever,
and that someday it will all be gone.

Bruce Smithhammer
The Words We Use

We have come to refer to rivers and forests, trout and elk as "resources." They have become units that inhabit still other units. We now frequently hear the act of hunting referred to as "harvesting" or "collection," or other, similarly clinical terminology. We have abstracted and reduced one of the most real, visceral experiences we have left in this modern world to the language of the bureaucrat and the commercial extractor.

There has, of course, been a necessity to this. In order to converse with the bureaucrat and the extractor, to be taken seriously and to have a seat at the table, it's become necessary to adopt their language, for this is the language that gets things done in our time. But in this linguistic shift, I believe something at the heart of this whole thing is lost, stripped of greater significance, reduced to the soulless level normally reserved for the inanimate product or commodity.

Wildlife managers, and some in the conservation profession, maintain that this is the required approach for science-based conservation, and in a broad, and regrettably bland and mechanical sense, they are absolutely correct. Management of wildlife, and wilderness, has largely become about numbers, stats, population counts, carrying capacities, "maximum sustainable yields" and the like.

It is not my goal to naively criticize this work, for I fully recognize its importance, just as I do its limitations. As mentioned above, statistics and quantifiable figures are essential in our day and age, if only in order to demonstrate value to a wider audience who apparently can value nothing else as highly. I know that this work is both important and well-intentioned. I support it as much as I possibly can, and am eternally grateful that there are those willing to fight the good fight on these stark terms.

Yet we also see this shift in language occur in yielding, consciously or otherwise, to societal pressures; to distance the dialogue surrounding hunting from being about something as disagreeable as "killing," and even from it being something that involves living, breathing beings at all. I suspect that these modifications in terminology are not coincidentally linked with greater shifting views in our culture toward hunting. How much easier, and more palatable, and less disruptive to the casual atmosphere of the cocktail party is it to say, in the presence of a hunting critic, that you spent the day "harvesting a local resource," than it is to say that you killed several quail or a deer? Pass the smoked salmon, would you?

"Language is not an abstract construction of the learned, or of dictionary makers, but is something arising out of the work, needs, ties, joys, affections, tastes, of long generations of humanity, and has its bases broad and low, close to the ground..." – Noah Webster

Is the recently dead grouse, whose warmth I can still feel through the game bag in the back of my vest, merely a "resource?" Moments ago, it was an eruption of wing and feather and cackle and native life. It will also soon be cooked as part of a special meal, relished as it should be, with respect for the life it was. To consider a wild river, or an expanse of old, healthy forest, and the marvelous things that inhabit these places, as mere "resources," or "units," would mean a fundamental part of me has withered and died. I know these places, and their inhabitants, too intimately to do them that disservice.

As a hunter and angler, deeply involved in this wet, dirty and sometimes bloody process, I have to draw a line and distance myself from this linguistic trend. This terminology can stay where it should in offices and negotiation rooms and urban environs. Words reflect how we perceive things, and I can't let the sterility of agency-speak infiltrate my own word choices. I can't consider the process of hunting and killing an animal as "resource collection," and I'm at a loss for what to say to anyone who has come to view this sacred, ancient act as anything so sterile. I won't distance myself from what this really is. It is hunting, and a part of hunting, at least sometimes, is taking a life. While this is far from the sole reason I am out here, neither is it a thing I take casually. Nor am I willing to trivialize or sanitize this act out of consideration for those who have become so removed from the fundamentals of natural processes, and the manner in which food arrives on their plates, that they can't deal with it. That is their burden to philosophically dance around, not mine.

Do you prefer to detach yourself from the singular act of having to kill what you eat? Does the reality of it make you squeamish or offend you, yet you still crave your burger or breast or steak? Well then it's easy—all too easy, really, and it comes in a plastic wrapped, styrofoam tray in the refrigerated section at your local grocery store. But don't try to drag me down that frigid, fluorescent-lit aisle with you.

Originally published on www.mouthfuloffeathers.com, Feb. 7, 2011

We Only Get So Many Octobers
Greg McReynolds

October is finite—not only in volume, but in reoccurrence.

In Idaho, October is the perfect month. The weather cools and the aspens start to drop their golden leaves. Brown trout move upstream to spawn, colored up like the aspens and hungry and edgy and mean. Sharp-tail seasons line up with other upland species so the whole host of bird hunting is on the menu.

October is a marker for my years, and sometimes it's alarming how fast they tick past. Throwing out a pair of worn out boots, I realize it's been a dozen years since I bought them. Sorting boxes of factory pheasant loads with $9 price tags, I try to remember when you could buy Golden Pheasant loads for that price.

Fondly remembering a hunt with a good friend, I realize we haven't spoken in years. I look at my dogs and see I no longer have one in her prime and one on the upswing, but one in her prime and one that may not have another October left in her.

For a good long time, I was certain my springer was faking deaf. As in, "I can't hear you boss, but there's birds!"

Turns out she is not faking, at least not anymore. Sometimes I walk past her bed and out the door without her waking. In the evening, I occasionally have to walk out and retrieve her from the yard. She's healthy and happy, but she has lost most of her drive and she can't hear anymore.

She'll make a few trips this year. Judging by our walks and initial trips out, she will mostly be at heel, strolling along as the old lady of the pack.

Last fall, I took an ill-advised shot at a rooster on the last day of the season. He seemed well hit, but locked his wings and glided across a good-sized channel of the Snake River into some cattails on the far shore. My old girl was never a good water retriever and I never force fetched her, but as I stood there wondering if my waders were in the truck, she lit out into the cold and fast water. She hit the shore and worked the cattails for several minutes before wading out and swimming back. She held a totally live rooster in her mouth, his head erect as she braved the current again.

I remember thinking, "That could be the last great retrieve I see her make," because even then she had slowed down. Mostly, the fire has gone out of her. She still wants to go, she wants to head out the door and ride in the truck, but the barely controlled bird craziness is gone. It's nice to have her around. She's mellowed. She can lie down at your feet instead of pacing constantly. She can ride in the car on a gravel road without howling to be let out.

She's just older. It happens to all of them. And to all of us. For me as well, there is a day coming where hunting turns into something else.

We only get so many Octobers.

Originally published on www.mouthfuloffeathers.com, Oct. 3, 2016

Thomas Reed
Liberty

Each morning now, I go somewhere I haven't been before. It's an easy, solo routine that asks no one for permission, checks in with no authorities, goes where it wants to go. I have a hunting license and I'm American, camping on American soil owned by every damned one of us.

There are but two limitations: obey the state's hunting laws and no camping in the same spot for more than sixteen days…as if I'd want to stay in one spot that long. I can live with those two rules.

The other rules are my own. Get up when I want, go when I want, shoot only a few birds out of each covey, treat my dogs well, leave enough for next time.

It has been this way for ten weeks now as I swing into the last two weeks of a three-month sabbatical from my real job. I have hunted five states, nine species of upland game birds, a dozen national forests, and thousands of acres of BLM ground. I asked no one for permission to go there, and I checked with myself to see if it was okay to go. It was. No one is more free.

It's a rare honor owned by only four percent of the world's population, we U.S. citizens. And were I less fortunate and had less than this chunk of time, I could still have gone. Gone for a weekend camping trip or an hour-long picnic with my family. It is as free a choice as deciding what side of the bed to sleep on.

In the evenings, I sit by the sharp clean burn of a hardwood campfire, smelling that good smoke, grilling my dinner. I sip corn liquor and pat my canine companions. I listen to coyotes talking from a near ridge, and far off on the skyline, I can see the lights of the city to the north. I read good books by flashlight and I stretch, take a few aspirin for middle-aged aches, and turn in. Then I do it all over again.

This is my liberty. Rise in the morning in the camper parked on American ground. Coffee, bacon, eggs. Breakfast done. Put the gun and the dogs in the truck. Load up on water and food for the day. Pull out the forest map and decide where I want to go. In a few weeks, my family will join me and we'll celebrate Christmas here. An outdoor Christmas with a nearby scraggly alligator juniper as our tree.

I'm only a few miles north of the border. Sometimes I wonder if anyone gets to hunt those beautiful oak slopes down in Mexico. I suspect not. It is likely owned by only one person while the ridge I'm standing alone on is owned by 320 million of us. Ironic that it feels in this moment as if I'm the only owner. Therein is the beauty of it.

I follow my little setter up onto benches of Spanish dagger and live oak. I drop into arroyos of granite and mesquite. I turn toward good-looking bird habitat when I see it. No one knows I'm out here. I'm free. Sometimes, I stop and rest against a boulder and I watch contrails in the sky and listen to Mabel's panting and think how damned fortunate I am to live in this country, with all of this American public land to hunt. Mostly, I just rest and think about nothing at all, which in this day and age is a good thing for someone who loves freedom and liberty. It is a good thing to get away from the raspy blather of the greedy.

I heard smatters of drivel coming from someone who has eyes on taking our American soil and turning it over to outside interests, claiming, incredulously, a constitutional right to such a theft from our people. "What price liberty?" asked the man with city-soft hands and never-seen-the-sun skin.

Try and take mine and you'll find out, I think, and I pick up my shotgun and follow my bird dog into another covey.

Originally published on www.mouthfuloffeathers.com, Mar. 24, 2016

Jillian Lukiwski
Seven Times Slower

On the first day of his fifteenth hunting season, Farley died in his sleep. Farley was our first gun dog, and when we brought him into our lives, I was ignorant as to how his life, bound to my own, would take me deeper into the landscapes I call home and deeper into the hearts and minds of all working dogs.

If you want to understand the magnificence of dogs as a unique species, hunt behind one. I once heard someone say the most disrespectful thing you can do to a dog is treat him like a human, and now I know those words to be true. In hindsight, I should have kicked off Farley's arrival with a heartfelt vow, earnest words spoken aloud for his ears and my own, something to capture the seriousness of the commitment I was taking on; but I didn't realize where this dog would lead my husband and me as individuals and as a family. A commitment to a gun dog is as serious as a marriage commitment except, thank goodness, a hunting collar is less expensive than a gold ring. Who of us is worthy of a good and stalwart pointing dog? None of us. We can only strive to be.

I didn't know what a German shorthaired pointer was when my husband told me he intended on procuring one. I took it upon myself to undergo a swift but thorough canine education. I made a journey to a good old-fashioned bookstore, whereupon I found a specific book about the dog breed my husband was so keen on. I read it cover to cover, on the spot. In the chapter that blathered on about breed standards, I saw the words, "A sign of good breeding is four lovely spoon-shaped feet." Someone had the audacity to describe the paws on these dogs as *lovely and spoon-shaped* and this specific detail appealed to my imagination to such a degree I converted immediately from being excited about any old mutt from the local pound to aligning myself with my husband's German shorthair dream.

We quickly located a breeder and sent a deposit for a male puppy. I was in Alaska when my husband made the journey alone across Arizona to pick the puppy up from the kennel. He chose a little male with a liver head and rump and a nearly-solid white body in between. For a few weeks I called home every day and begged Robert to tell me stories about the puppy I hadn't yet seen. We tried to name him, but everything we came up with failed to suit the pup. Even at eight weeks old he had a distinct personality.

One day, over the phone, my husband suggested the name Farley in honor of the beloved Canadian author, Farley Mowat. Robert tried the name out on the puppy and it stuck. Farley would turn out to be sweet, smart, dorky and idiosyncratic in rather endearing ways. I would like to think that Mr. Mowat would be honored.

At last, I flew home from the dewy-fresh summer of Alaska to the dry-blaze of Arizona, burst in the front door of the house to announce my arrival and there, in the hallway, was the floppiest puppy I had ever seen. In absolute elation I hollered, "Farley!" Farley took one look at me, peed himself, and ran to the far end of the house where he hid beneath the sofa while whining and shaking.

I despaired; my puppy feared me. I quietly sidestepped the puddle, walked to the end of the house, assumed a quadruped position and peered beneath the furniture. I spoke quietly, convincingly to Farley, and eventually he emerged, sniffed me all over and waggled his docked tail until I thought his body might fall to pieces, like a jalopy on an eternal stretch of washboard road. I picked him up and held him to me, he pushed his face into the curve of my neck; his girl had come home.

He tore our lives apart for a little while. If I'm honest, he tore it apart for the better part of his first four years. We once made the mistake of leaving him sleeping on his dog bed while we ran to town for tacos, and when we returned it looked like an F4 tornado had ripped through the house. Plants were unearthed from their pots and flung about the living room, Jackson Pollock style. The kitchen garbage had also succumbed to his wild anxiety, and he took great care to not only empty it entirely, but also to stash the addled contents in every nook and cranny in the house—I found a petrified banana peel seven months later beneath the shoe rack.

Farley himself was standing atop the kitchen table, spraddle legged as a giraffe at a watering hole, his little pink tongue licking the butter. He paused then, there in the eye of the storm, looked at us with joy on his face, waggled his stubby tail like a maniac—delighted by our return—and then he resumed sweeping his tongue across the salty lump of gold. Thus began his lifelong love of butter.

Do dogs, like cats, have nine lives to live? Farley didn't have nine lives to live, but he certainly had more than one to squander. In Arizona I once watched him launch himself over a creosote bush and was horrified to see a rattlesnake shoot upwards from where it was coiled on the ground, fangs unsheathed and gleaming with malice. Scaled lightning. Thankfully, the trajectories between dog and rattler were incompatible. Farley flew over the snake like a sleek, metallic aircraft in a tactical maneuver. He let out a surprised yelp at the apex of his flight, continued soaring through the air in a perfect parabolic arc, and landed safely on the other side, unbitten, unscathed, undeterred. I breathed a sigh of relief. Farley kept on running with his nose to the wind.

Farley loathed skunks with the fire of a thousand burning suns, and has been sprayed more often than any other dog we've ever known. In fact, if you tally up the skunk spritzes endured by all six dogs we've owned, Farley still comes out like an indomitable champion in the lead. I once watched Farley catch a skunk by the arse and proceed to chew on it like it was a rubber squeaky toy for the better part of three minutes. Let me tell you, one hundred and eighty seconds can tick by quite slowly in such dire circumstances. I pleaded with Farley to spit the skunk out and he refused, blinded and deafened by his hatred for Pepé Le Pew. The skunk's feet paddled the air like an olympic swimmer while its rear end attended to the business of emptying skunk essence, squirt by squirt, directly into Farley's outraged mouth. The malodorous attempt at self-defense seemed to only make the dog angrier. The intensity of Farley's rage visibly doubled, and there wasn't a thing I could do about it.

At close range, the fumes were unbelievably potent. The stink drew tears from my eyes and my palate became offended by the swirl of rank molecules. Farley continued to crush the skunk's rear quarters with a fervor I haven't seen in any dog since, eventually doing enough internal damage that the skunk died.

Once the varmint was defeated, Farley spat the limp body into a sagebrush, hunched over, and promptly began one straight hour of violent vomiting. For the better part of the next week he struggled to consume any food, so corroded was his gut by skunk spray. I wish I could tell you he learned a lesson, but his intolerance of skunks was something of a holy crusade. He continued to toy with them into old age.

One year, in a two-month span, Farley set his mouth on four different porcupines and the vet bills threatened to bankrupt us. His final encounter resulted in an infection in his nose. Short on cash as we were at the time, we took care of him the country way and proceeded to the ranch supply, purchased a bottle of antibiotics intended for treating cattle, dosed it down to his weight, and treated the infection with immediate success. At the end of it all the single, troublesome quill that caused the kerfuffle in the first place finally worked its way up through the roof of his mouth and out through the top of his nose—poking out like a church steeple on an expanse of prairie. When I grasped that final, pesky quill with the Leatherman pliers and steadily pulled until it popped out, I can testify we were all in the grip of rapturous relief.

I won't claim that Farley was the best pointing dog ever to walk the face of Earth, but he was a master, a real Leonardo da Vinci of dogs. His hunting repertoire included fifteen upland bird species, and he made himself handy on geese and ducks in the blind from time to time. He was also known to subsidize his daily food requirements by digging up and eating alive dozens of voles a day in our hayfield, making him a more valuable mouser than my three barn cats combined.

It wasn't until the event we call "The Big Fetch" that I began to truly understand Farley and appreciate his character and drive. We were hunting quail in a wide, creosote-studded wash, and followed Farley's nose to the top of an adjacent mesa where he hit a lovely point. My husband flushed the birds and peppered one hard enough that we saw it flinch in flight before the covey dropped off the mesa edge and out of sight. Farley went ripping past us, and like the Man From Snowy River on a sturdy brumby, he dove off the mesa and galloped nose-first down the nearly ninety-degree cliff face. All that was missing from the scene was the report of a bullwhip cracking.

He reached the wash at the bottom of the cliff and continued chasing the covey across the sand. From our vantage we watched as the quail continued flying across the flat expanse with Farley closing the distance with greedy, ground-devouring strides. He drew closer to the wounded quail, which was still flying, but failing. To our shock, he leaped off the ground and fetched the fatigued bird out of the air. Its final wing beats smacked him in the jowls. He landed on all fours, quail secure in his maw, smartly turned and began a relaxed lope back across the wash to the base of the mesa. There he engaged his four-by-four, clambered up the nearly-sheer cliff face, popped out on top and deposited the quail in my husband's hand.

Tongue fully extended and dripping with exertion, Farley flopped down in the dirt to rest.

This was when I realized our dog had heart and charisma and an unsurpassed devotion—to us, of course, but more importantly, to his work. I have never seen another pointing dog perform such an uncanny retrieve. The event was in the realm of the supernatural; it's still difficult to fathom and believe. We hunted him for another fourteen years, and he always gave the field the fullness of his effort and attention. I can tell you without a doubt thar his work fulfilled him in a way that few humans or dogs ever achieve. He felt great affection for us, but he loved his work, and I was never jealous. For a gundog, this is exactly how love should be.

The best lesson Farley ever taught me was that developing a gun dog is not about controlling their every movement in the field. The goal is not to be a fiendish master ruling over a cowering, slavish creature, but to be strong and kind, to teach a pup the value of self-control and composure, and to mirror that same demeanor and character at home and in the field.

Farley also taught me that a good hunting dog has the opportunity to achieve greatness when his handler learns the dog's language, when the dog is permitted to communicate and to be heard. A dog cannot say in the language of man, "There's a single quail holding at the roots of that sagebrush on the southside of this spring creek." But I can watch him track foot scent with his nose close to the ground while he waggles his tail with exuberance, and I can watch him bring his nose up when he catches a pungent whiff of body scent on the breeze. I can see him work the field in decreasing arcs as his speed slows and he begins to creep and stalk and stand his game. I can watch all of his subtle body language with great expectations, and when I see his eyes blazing like a hay barn on fire in the night, his body freezes as though he has been chiseled from marble by deft hands. I can interpret quite clearly that he is locked onto and holding a group of birds. My job is simply to observe and keep up with him until he conveys to me with every muscle, sinew and bone to get the shotgun ready, flick the safety off and blast him a doggone bird.

Farley taught me the language of pointing dogs which I speak fluently, still. He also transcribed for me a bigger lesson, a lesson on the topic of the ineffable. He wrote it on my heart with indelible ink. I keep my ego in check by remembering this: *I follow my dogs* into the field. A dog hunts into the wind and ushers me onward. I go where he goes; I follow where he leads.

I am haunted by a poetic line in Psalm 42, "the deep calls out to deep". Companionship with a dog is a pleasure to experience, but a true partnership with a gun dog causes the unfathomable depths of my person to call out to and plumb the immeasurable universe of another living thing. Deep calls out to deep, and when I listen intuitively with all of my cells to the mysterious *thing* that exists within us all, sometimes I get lucky and the deep answers the deep.

I am tirelessly hunting for what is real and true in this life. Occasionally it's the wise, curious nose of a gun dog that leads me to questions I never asked and answers I never knew I was seeking, ultimately launching me out of the synthetic shallows of the modern world into a raw, tender, untrammeled wilderness that eternally awaits me.

Farley grew old. For every day he hunted, he ached and limped for three. His bones creaked like hardwood floors when he stood up from his bed, his face turned silver, arthritic mice scurried about in his joints, his eyes lost their sharpness—but his nose still worked. We had a second shorthair by that time and whenever we left Farley home to rest and recover from the hunt the day before, he made a sorrowful ruckus, voicing his absolute denial of his physical limitations until so wrung out by his woe, he lay back down in his bed to sleep until our return.

It's hard to watch a good dog grow old. Jim Harrison reminds us, "in the main we only die seven times slower than our dogs," and watching Farley move into the twilight of his life broke my heart for us all it broke my heart that all this vigor, all this beauty and youth and stamina, all the vitality and aliveness in the world cannot last forever: not his, not the wildflowers,' not my own.

Farley died alone. While we were away, our farm-sitter called to inform us Farley had curled up outside on the hard concrete of our dog run, shut his eyes to sleep, and failed to wake up. The weather was rotten with heat and we couldn't travel home immediately, so a kind neighbor buried him for us five feet deep. I missed the opportunity to enact the ceremony I perform when my animals die and I lay their heavy, spiritless bodies in a hand-dug grave. I failed to be there to make Farley comfortable in his last hours, to stroke his face, to help him let go peacefully. I have carried a portion of guilt for a couple years; I failed my gun dog in his time of need. There is grace and mercy in remembrance, and the story of Farley I keep in my heart is one of love, trust, hilarity and grit.

Each time we set Farley on the ground and spoke the incantation to hunt, we asked him to lead us onward and we trusted in his leadership. We proceeded into the vast unknown of the landscape, of ourselves, of him, with fidelity stuck to our souls like November's mud clinging to our boots. Farley was the first of us to move through life and set his feet down on the other side of death, and in that regard, he continues to lead us still. I know he'll stand his game and hold his point—as we always trusted him to, as he always did—until we join him there.

Ryan Busse
Born of a Barstool

It was a small-town, western Montana watering hole, the kind of bar where patrons gathered after work to toss peanut shells into sawdust and share their lives with friends over cheap beers. I did not know a soul in the place and had yet to make a friend in this new town despite my attempts to find someone who shared a passion for bird hunting. And then one random night, like drifting covey scent through tall grass, I caught hints of interesting stories drifting over the beer from a loud guy at the end of the bar.

The fella floating the words had folded his six-foot, five-inch frame onto a random barstool. He wore a Stormy Kromer wool hat, just like the ranchers I grew up with, and his pontifications gained volume and color with each swig of his beer.

He had a particular way of speaking. Plain and authoritative; in the style of a stern traveling preacher minus any hint of piety. His voice was slow and booming, and his words were laced with a Canadian accent and contained unique off-color colloquialisms that echoed off the low ceiling.

It was a risk, but obviously, this guy hunted, and I needed a buddy who knew the country, so I leaned toward him and took a chance with a playful challenge, "What do you know about pheasants?" He stopped mid-sentence and shot back a retort, "Quite a goddamned bit. I'm James. Who the hell are you?"

James had been delivering a stirring sermon about a recent pheasant trip he'd taken. Despite holding peanuts in one hand and beer in the other, he waved his arms around as if in a pulpit. His parishioners around the bar listened with rapt attention: "They were flying around like goddamned bees. Everywhere! We were shootin' the hell outta things, the dogs were crazy as shithouse rats and the birds were piling up like cordwood." My intrusion brought that all to an uncomfortable standstill.

I had grown up on a ranch with more pheasants than we could count. Hunting access to my childhood home seemed like currency I could use in barter and so

I offered him a handshake and a follow-up. "You think you know what pheasant hunting is? Well you ought to see where I grew up."

James bore a strong resemblance to the iconic Major League pitcher Randy Johnson. As he stood and looked down his nose with a cocked eyebrow, I felt as if I was standing at home plate with the Big Unit staring me down, shaking his head as he took signs from the catcher. But he opted for no brushback pitch, and after a few seconds, he shook my hand and told the bartender to "Get this guy a beer."

For James, a hint of wild birds on a big ranch was intriguing enough to explore friendship with a stranger. A few months later, Jim and his dog were strolling across the grasslands of our ranch in the biting cold. Never mind the 1,200-mile drive or the uncertainty of being in an unknown place with a guy he just met. I had a lot of respect for that sort of gamble, because it's just exactly the sort I would have taken.

Our hunting styles were a match too. I loved to cover miles, and James was a born walker. Like a moose at a long distance, he first seemed slow and gangly. But up close he moved across bird country with stretched, effortless strides, so long and flowing that almost no one could keep up. When birds appeared, he'd swing, shoot, and take a new step all in the same motion, never stopping his forward momentum.

Like me, Jim possessed an uncommon internal bird hunting drive. Twenty-mile days and hunting right up until dusk became common. Before long, other friends labeled our adventures as "death marches," and sought excuses to avoid getting looped into our hikes. None of that phased us. We just kept on hunting.

Our shared passion for birds and our dogs drove us to range over huge swaths of country together. In the ensuing decades, we hunted and explored the high plains from Oklahoma to Canada. In the times between our marches, we found small towns, snuck dogs into dingy hotels, and ate breakfasts in greasy spoons.

We listened to the conversations of old men in cafes on the off chance they might utter a tip about birds on their farms. We chatted up crusty bartenders to find out what whiskey important ranchers drank. We lived it all with unapologetic abandon, and our experiences proved to be valuable ingredients in Jim's art.

I grew to know him as a master of storytelling. Our adventures became threads in his projects. He picked out the interesting places and people and then wove them in the loom of his mind, spinning them together until the fine fabric poured out.

His stories almost always arrived at unexpected and hilarious places. "Did I ever tell you about the time I took out an entire motel in a runaway grain truck?" Turns out he had done just that. The roadside lodging establishment was thankfully almost empty due to the late morning timing of his crash, but Jim's loaded wheat truck nearly killed the last person inside just as she was preparing to check out of room 107. He, too, barely made it out alive. The motel itself was not so lucky, and the story about it all was priceless.

A few years after the wreck, and in classic Jim fashion, he randomly met the survivor on the same barstool where he and I had first discussed pheasants. Of course, he started preaching and drinking beer with her, too. They ended up laughing over another of Jim's stories even though she was minus a few key internal organs due to the impact of the 40-ton grain truck. He had almost killed the gal with his Peterbilt, but that did not stop him from inquiring about the possibility of gaining permission to hunt on any property she or her family might own.

Jim wove the words of his life together with the magnetic pull of the world's finest novelists. Before long, his storytelling was in high demand by my friends and family. Inquiries about upcoming hunting trips soon focused on whether James was coming along. It was his attendance that would make or break the trip.

The truth is that James was simply the kind of guy you wanted to have along for the ride. For me, this was at least partially because he was particularly silver-tongued when prying permission from even the prickliest ranchers. Given my fluency in ranch language, I thought I was pretty good at the permission game, but I had to admit he might have been the best I have ever seen.

After a hard, "No. We don't allow hunting," through the screen door, Jim would build up to another of his booming sermonettes. He began with something familiar: commentary on a truck, or a cow, or the weather. Then he worked towards an artful transition to a real or imagined memory of a distant cousin they both knew who maybe went to school with a friend, or a last name that sounded about right, and then he'd throw in a good joke and one of his unique descriptive terms.

Soon the door would creak open, and Jim was inside, drinking coffee, eating cookies and drawing property maps on paper towels. A warm handshake from the previously frigid rancher, then he'd swagger back to the truck with his wool hat tipped just so, a slight grin creeping up from his mustache. After his truck door slammed he'd unleash the results: "Hope you got some goddamned ammo Busse, 'cause we can hunt 'er all!"

Shaking my head in amazement, we'd drive off, soon to begin marching across another swath of prairie while shooting at those birds that would surely be flying around like the bees in his stories.

Those ranchers sensed what I already knew: you could depend on Jim to be true and authentic. He became a cornerpost in the wobbly fence of my life. Something steady and predictable. Over time, things got busier, and I traveled more. Life happened. We hunted together less, but that did not matter to the fundamentals of our friendship. On one of my work trips, my wife Sara called me to explain that our beloved Shorthair, with whom I had hunted nearly 16 years, was on her last leg. Our vet advised us to put her down that same day. I could not return for nearly a week. In tears, I blubbered into the phone, "I'll call James."

Of course, he dropped everything and was at Sara's side within the hour as we lost a bird dog. He cried in the waiting room just as I would have for his dogs. He thought nothing of doing it and by now, it's probably woven into another of his colorful stories.

When our first son was born, Sara and I named him Lander James, in honor of one of our favorite Wyoming places and my friend James. Lander was born in the middle of Jim's January duck hunting, but he took the interruption in stride, showing up at the hospital in camo while promising to take the infant to a new spot that he declared, "had a shitload of ducks when things froze up like this."

Nearly 25 years have now passed since our first beers together in that bar. We've walked a thousand miles, together and apart. New dogs have come and gone. Birds have indeed been piled up like cordwood. Family has passed, and a son has been named in his honor. And yet, despite that long march of time, it is as if nothing at all has changed. We are just a couple of bird-hunting buddies looking for the next ridge to hunt and tale to weave. We joke with each other about missed shots and permissions gained. It's a friendship between men based on the most elementary components, first brought together by a random encounter and a shared desire to find new bird country.

We don't waste time discussing the fates or wondering why it happened, because all we have ever done is follow our dogs and tell stories. These are simple things that are enough for us.

The Old Man's Gun
Thomas Reed

On the first day of the last month of the year, the old man rose from his sleep and shuffled into winter. The Jefferson River lay just west, frozen mute in his Montana, and the wind was building in the willows and cottonwoods as a cold sun—its light not even a promise at this hour—started to creep up the far side of a mountain called Manhead.

He had lived past his friends and had lived it full. He had outlasted all his old hunting partners and lost touch with a few more whom he was certain he had also outlasted. A dozen gun dogs, a dozen horses, three wives. He had shot a Featherweight Model 70 enough to have to replace its barrel, and before that rifle, a Model 54 in .270 had been shot so much and developed throat-wobble so badly that he had a gunsmith rebore the gun into the Colonel Townsend's legendary .35 Whelen. He'd ridden a saddle made in Denver by the famous maker Heiser through its first sheepskin and a couple latigos. His best gun, a Browning Superposed he had carried across the uplands of the West, was in need of its second refurbishing.

He lived all on his own, but not alone. He spoke to his old setter, Pat, and brushed her soft head with a kind hand and told her to lie back down in her room.

In his other hand was a cheap pistol, a .380 of brutish manufacture he had purchased at a gun show, a throw-away, a gun no one would want, especially after. Two gun safes were full of the other kinds of guns—the legendary, the crafted, the collectors. The Superposed was on loan to me.

***

Jim Houston first laid eyes on the Superposed 20 in a Denver pawn shop. It was 1966 and the image of it standing there delicate and balanced and perfect among clunky pumps and choppy-lined side-by-sides seared itself into his brain. The shopkeeper stood firm at two hundred-twenty-five dollars for the beautiful shotgun made in Belgium in 1953. Two hundred-twenty-five dollars for a 20 gauge shotgun was a lot on a game warden's salary at a time when the average new car sold for just a touch over three-thousand dollars. But by the time Jim had driven the five hours back to his warden station in Colorado's San Juan, he had figured how to sell enough deer hides he salvaged from road- and winter-killed deer to afford it. At home, he urged an old college buddy in the city to visit the pawn shop, and the shotgun was his.

I know this story by heart. I have heard this story over the span of better than thirty years, over elk tacos and caribou loin, over martinis and margaritas and bacon-wrapped quail grilled on mesquite coals in some lonely desert. Masters have a way of telling stories again and again and again that move the listener to yearn for the retelling, the story itself held in reverence in its repetition. The virtuoso raconteur will paint and play act, transport and bring to life. Jim is one of these, his well-bottom-deep voice raising and lowering, conveying emotion—mirth, surprise, disgust—anything needed to spice the story.

Blended into this grand presentation is his knowledge of wild country, bird dogs, horses, guns, history, current affairs, literature. Each taken individually is enough to captivate. His stories, such as how he purchased the beautiful shotgun on a thin salary as a young warden with a family, flavor and highlight each of our many trips together: trips in high country and desert, field and prairie, canyon and mesa. All in pursuit of game and fish and often following a fine-flowing English setter into a beckoning wind.

He carried the Superposed though these years and I have seen this gun swing on the quail of the southwest, the chukar of the high desert, the sharptail of the great American prairies, blue grouse against the tall big sky, cackling brilliant pheasants, Huns buzzing in a single burst to the pale blue. I have seen the arc of this gun in all weather and all places. The gun that stood as clean and lean and beautiful as a thoroughbred's flank in a kill pen of culls that was a Denver pawn shop, the gun that was John Browning's last genius, the gun that turned the upland world on its head in the 1930s and revolutionized the single-trigger double gun industry; that challenged the orientation of barrels and the idea of repeaters.

This beautiful September morning in 1988, the gun is cased in a leather scabbard on Jim's well-used Heiser saddle aboard a Missouri Fox Trotter horse named Todd. I'm on a big gray horse named Mike; my own shotgun, a Browning Citori made in Japan, cased in its own scabbard. We are following Jim's two setters, Ned and Jed, across a wide sage-covered mountain north of Gunnison, Colorado, in pursuit of sage and blue grouse. Ned is a tri-color coming into late middle age and moving like it, but the younger dog, Jed, is a blue belton, and watching him flow across the landscape is like watching clear, cold water flowing from the toe of a glacier. It is more dance than gallop, a waltz that the young setter follows with the wind supplying tempo and cadence.

Jim and I have known each other now for less than a year but there is a comfort here between mentor and protégé. I don't think about the fact that he is my father's age, and that perhaps I'm substituting, attaching myself to a father figure who has deep passions for the same things that have captured me since youth. I'll let the psychologists work that one out, for my own blood father and I share other passions, and even if he is not a man of the outdoors, I love him dearly. Jim has a son not much older than I am, but like my father, his passions lie elsewhere than bird dogs, horses, good guns, and tall country. The psychologists might find this paradigm useful for citation in a study of father-son relationships of some kind, both of us substituting somehow. But no matter. We are hunting.

Hunting is what I wake up after dreaming of all night. Hunting, and fishing, gather all my attention, even when I am forced to do other work to earn my living. I am the editor of a small town Rocky Mountain newspaper, but it is hunting that I'd rather be doing, and here on this gray horse in September in the Rockies, I'm high with it.

My own bird dog, a mutt named JD—half Labrador and half Springer Spaniel—is at home because she is a flusher where Ned and Jed are pointers, but truth be told, it goes deeper than that. I know that I am gravitating toward setters for the rest of my life, even though this is our first hunt. It's in the watching of it, the beauty of two professionals doing their thing, guided by instinct and breeding and scent. My God, I think, here I am on a horse with a gun following a bird dog on a September morning, full of everything a 20-something can be full of—probably mostly himself. This: this is being alive.

I have read outdoor stories of the uplands where the author writes the line "Jake goes on point."
These four words are as lacking in detail as to be criminal. It's like describing Norman Mailer's 1,136 page *The Executioner's Song* as a book about a guy who gets shot by a firing squad. Watching a dog pivot into a wind, finding the edge of scent

plume, spinning back into the stronger current, then tightening his entire body from the very tip of his nose to the last hair on his tail, creeping, easing panther-like, whispering into the deep windstorm of scent. There is so much more there than, "Jake goes on point."

At a place where a gully rises up and over onto a small bench, Jed does just this while Ned, off on his own scent stream, pays little attention to his younger companion. Watching all of this from Todd's back, Jim shouts: "Ned. Whoa" then looks at me, disgust in his voice. "Ned has no honor in him." But the dog does stop and Jim looks at me. Jed is frozen off to my right and I can see Jim's eyebrows lift beneath his Stetson before he says, "Jed's got them. You got this one."

As with the best teachers, Jim expects the student to have some bit of self-start, some inkling of independence without paint-by-numbers instruction and—a trait I credit to learning from my own father—I do. I step off, then look around, wondering what to do with the horse's reins. Jim sees this too without me asking and says, "Just drop them. He's trained and he won't go far even if he decides to get silly." So I do, and I yank the Citori from the scabbard, thumb it open and quickly stuff in two shells. Then I walk in.

I have spent my entire college career hunting the tiny rocket that is the quail of the southwest. On winter breaks back home in Colorado, I have downed rooster pheasants by the cooler-full. I've shot the Citori enough to think I kind of know how to shoot. None of this prepares me for what is about to happen.

The dog, the sky, the horses behind me, my new friend in his cowboy hat looking on from the back of a bay horse, the town whose newspaper I edit far in the southern distance, all of it. Then all of it shatters as if the entire sky has fragmented into feathers climbing through clear air. Seven or eight huge birds loft to the heavens as one. Gunners have described the sage grouse's launch to the great beyond in many ways—World War II bombers and the less flattering flying trashcan lid—but in this moment, all I know is that they are huge and seem pretty damned fast and the gun is on my shoulder and talking. And that I miss. Twice. I'm not sure how. Seems as if a guy could just shoot his gun off in the air randomly and hit one, they are so big. But I've missed. At the shot, Jed breaks and rips after the flock—covey too delicate a word for birds of this bulk—but nothing falls. I didn't even come close. I turn back to the horses and my friend and he is chuckling quietly, which pisses me off and wounds my pride, but then his words ease it all.

"We will find more."

We do. This wide mountain, this expanse of sage and aspen and chokecherry is ours and we twist across it, dropping into long drainages, climbing up onto benches, following the wind that leads the dogs. They point again, both of them this time, and Jim is off Todd before I can even pull Mike up, and the birds are up and I watch him there in his tan shooting jacket and matching Stetson, the gun to his shoulder in perfect form and the pop of the Superposed twice. Two sage grouse stagger in flight, fold up like lawn chairs and plummet to the ground and the dogs, each of them with a bird, come roaring back with the big chickens nearly covering their eyes. Jim is chortling and kneeling and talking, joy in his voice, joy wagging and twisting the dogs into knots.

This day changes everything. Astride September wonder, the dogs afore, the guns often uncased from saddle scabbard, the scent of sage and horse, leather and autumn aspen. Gunpowder. We do not talk much, my new friend and I. Mostly we watch the dogs and I watch the man. The course of my young life forever altered.

***

Perhaps because I first hunted the American southwest where the great Apache chief Cochise once hunted, I cannot think about Arizona and New Mexico, cannot step onto her granite skin, walk among agave and cholla, over cold lava and warm sand, without thinking of civilizations and cultures. All of them, from Conquistador to Comanche and Apache, cowboy, vaquero. It is a desert, to be sure, but it is a diverse land with a half dozen life zones in as many crow-flies miles and people from all corners. It is little surprise that Jim and I in our early months of get-to-know-you conversation discover a mutual love of chilles rellenos, bunkhouse honkytonks and desert quail.

This lands us here, against a sunlit stone mountain where the Apache once camped, with our wives on this warm January day in 1993. Kelly and I have driven down from Cheyenne, Wyoming, a bitter, bland refinery town on the edge of the Rockies. Jim and his wife came down from Gunnison where Jim in "retirement" runs The Book Worm Book Store—New and Used Books • Specializing In Outdoor Subjects • All Local Maps In Stock • Free Backcountry Advice—which is where he met and fell in love with Susan.

Here and now our camp is stunningly beautiful—Jim and Susan's trailer and our nylon tent—beneath the spreading limbs of an Emery oak, backed up against a granite monolith as big as a county courthouse, looking east toward a whole mountain of stone that is baking to a nice orange in the falling sunlight of a day. Some years after this first camp, I will arrive with my own setter, Hank, at this same place to meet Jim and while I wait, a film crew and a beautiful woman will arrive and drive east toward the rock where for the next hour, the woman will pose naked on slabs of sun-warmed stone to the frenetic click of the photographer's camera in plain sight of camp. Jim will find me here with binoculars, a beer and a forgotten cigar sometime later.

After the cold wind of the Wyoming prairie, the warmth of a southwestern sun on winter shoulder and Vitamin D-starved skin feels almost sinfully good. Jim and Susan discovered this camp of all camps a few years back in a rare blizzard when they climbed off the valley of the San Pedro, dropped the Ford into four-wheel-drive, and punched through a foot of fresh powder. When the tires lost traction, Jim, ever the prepared, chained up the rear wheels and kept going until a faint two-track appeared, and the Ford and its camper floated sleigh-like in the white-out to this very place.

They woke on Christmas Eve morning to a foot of fresh powder covering oak, granite and agave. Jim stepped into this scene with the Superposed in a gloved hand and Jed and Ned flung outward. In an hour or two, with a half-limit of Mearns quail warm against the small of his back, he was back at the camper for a late breakfast with his wife.

This year the land is the same but the weather is much different. The warmth and glow of it seems to come from everywhere: the rock, the sky, the sun, the company. Mostly the company. We followed Jim's precise directions and here we are. In the morning it will be quail, but before the light is out of the sky for the day and we dig into the evening meal, Jim and Susan beckon us west of camp. There they show us a place where a half-dozen or more Apache—Cochise's people—knelt before bowls of stone called *metates* worn deep in a huge slab. We stand in the silence thinking of *mano* grinding on *metate*, the busy chatter of a people somehow long gone but still here. The sun drops out of the sky and the granite turns pale lavender.

To my mind, there is no beauty like the subtle beauty of a Mearns quail in hand. It is the mix of it all—the grass, the oak, the dog, the gun, the feel of all of these cultures in an open heart. The tamales purchased from a woman who has a cooler full of them for sale in the post office parking lot of a southeastern Arizona widespot, the chilies bought at the New Mexico roadside stand, the pinto beans from the big farm down near Lordsburg—the whole God-damned glorious fullness of it. Hold this little beautiful quail for a moment and see this, male or female: browns and blacks and sorrel, whites. Perhaps because my favorite color on a horse is bay—black legs, mane, tail and deep mahogany coat—the Mearns, especially the mature male of the species, well, that's about as beautiful a creature as the Creator ever created. Or then again, maybe it's the whole experience that is hunting in shirtsleeves in January desert warmth while back home it's forty below.

Jim and I find ourselves walking behind Jed into the heart of Mearns country the next day. Ned is pretty much done, cataracted and arthritic and enjoying the warmth of an affectionate friend in Susan. JD the flusher will stay behind this time too. I have been reading voraciously of setters and miraculously seeing them in nearly every piece of sporting artwork I lay eyes upon. Kelly has accepted that there will be a setter in our future someday. But for now, I follow Jed, and between the two of us, he floats through the grass. When the cowboys discovered this part of the great southwest with its wide-open spaces nearly waist-high in grass, oaks scattered for shade from a summer sun, water seeping from granite here and there, they thought they had discovered bovine heaven. But this is still a desert and many a bankrupt would-be cattleman then and since has realized the delicateness of the place and how quickly tall grass can evaporate into that four-chambered gullet and the land go to bare dirt. Mearns, Gambel, and scaled quail all live here and their populations are as mercurial and fickle as summer, spring or even winter rain. This is an up year.

I'm carrying the Citori and its 12 gauge strength seems a bit much for these little birds. Jim, of course, has the Superposed and by the time we walk, hours later, back to the pickup truck from a tangled ravine that went on for miles, then back down the adjoining one, we both have a handful of quail in our vests and both are tired, cat-clawed, mesquite-thorned and happy. Tonight there will be quail and just a small slice of jalapeno wrapped in bacon grilled over the coals of mesquite harvested two steps away from our tent. Tomorrow, perhaps, more of the same, if we are living right and somehow, I think we are: the four of us with our laughter bouncing off Cochise's stone fortress.

***

Chukar hunting demands much of leg and lung, and it will be the first to end. The sheer, brute physicality of it, climbing a country laid on end, over slick stone and boot-grabbing sagebrush. There's a saying among those who climb, the mountaineers: There are old mountaineers and bold mountaineers but there are no old, bold mountaineers. There are very few old chukar hunters, bold or otherwise.

This is basic doctrine of the chukar bulwark as is one other: this is no place for a double gun. I have tried. Carried the faithful, and now well-used Citori high and low, then thought I needed to be a bit more tweedy and switched to a side-by-side Ithaca Flues 16 with double triggers. This, after reading some bard of the crags claim he was adept enough to shoot the full choke trigger at a long flusher or the modified trigger at a close-riser, something I should have had the common sense to realize I had neither the iron nerve—many a flushing chukar has so surprised me that I've nearly pooped my pants as my young son would say—nor the quick wittedness to pull off. Plus, the Ithaca had been chopped short to accommodate a much smaller gunner and when Jim held the gun to his shoulder one evening in his camp trailer after a particularly frustrating day of point-bang-bang-damnit, point-bang-bang-damnit, *ad nauseam*, he merely said, "It would be tough to hit anything with this gun." So it is best to admit this outright: chukar partridge is the bird that turned me into a shameless autoloader man. The reason is simple. Three shots instead of two.

No bird on this planet sparks bloodlust quite like the chukar of our northern deserts, and for all the cliché reasons, their running, their propensity to flush behind you, to flush far ahead of you, to fly out of range, to climb a mountain before you can tighten your boots at the pickup truck, or the all-time worst: to flush below you and peel left or right while rapidly dropping elevation. This latter shot is the most difficult of the uplands, the down, dropping and away, a shot that is usually checked by the bird hunter not wanting to shoot the top of his dog's head off, or just the inability of most to swing shotgun across and down from an elevated position rather than across and up or level. The chukar partridge is the lone bird of the uplands, save perhaps the rooster pheasant, where the triumphant trumpet of the successful gunner is "got that bastard" rather than "what an honor it is to kill such a beautiful creature." Finally, I should mention the tendency of the chukar partridge to a) flush and the chukar hunter to b) empty his gun at the covey rise and the remaining one or two or three chukar to c) flush again and the chukar hunter to d) curse a blue streak over his broken open and empty double gun. So I became an autoloader man.

Naturally, Jim defies the two principles of the precipice and on this late November night in 2003, the camp trailer tucked up under a juniper tree in the middle of a lonely Nevada desert beneath a sage-rimmed canyon, I tease him for defying the age rule—he is in his 70s now, and we just spent a day together climbing up a broken slab of a mountain that time was slowly taking to pieces, much like an earthquake might take apart a pottery shop. Plus he was carrying the Superposed, two shots, but also a gun so beautiful that carrying it over rough terrain is a bit like carrying a raw egg in a spoon on a highwire. Most of the veteran chukar hunters not only carry autoloaders, they also carry butt-ugly autoloaders with composite stocks of camo or black, not pretty and historic guns stocked in English walnut where a fall might do permanent damage to both gun and hunter. Chukar hunting is hard on both man and gun. One year Jim and I walked into a gray day that turned into a sideways blizzard that pounded us all afternoon. When we returned to the trailer for warmth and a toddy and just plain survival, we each were covered in ice and snow, as were the bird dogs and Jim's Superposed and my Citori. Nevada has a way of just going ahead and killing you rather than some kind of slow torture. This, though, was not enough for Jim to case the Superposed for good and try one of the other guns in his quiver. He merely wiped it off, found an oil cloth and wiped it off again and stored it for use the next day. I followed suit with my own double.

Life, like Nevada weather, has a way of just going ahead and getting it done. Kelly and I divorced years ago and Jim and Susan sold the bookshop and everything else and moved to a beautiful little farm in Montana. I moved from Cheyenne to Lander and back to Cheyenne. Bird dogs and horses for both of us have come and gone, and the "campfire advice" has turned to women along with bird dogs, horses and guns. Jim has listened to a sad lament or two in the country-song life of a single man that I'm living, but mostly it is just the land, the birds, the sky, the guns and the dogs. Jim's game warden stories, of course, follow us to the high elk and grouse camps of Wyoming, the prairies of the Dakotas and

Montana, the broken sagebrush sea of Idaho and Nevada, and back to Arizona's quail country.

This crumpled country with its sage and obsidian, its coveys of Huns and quail in canyon mouths and laughing chukar on rimrock, anchors us solidly here at this camp for the better part of two weeks. At night, we burn old sage and juniper in a crackling campfire against November, and we compare notes of our day. The next morning, I climb a slab of cold lava slowly being beaten down by the inexorable march of time and its henchmen: water, wind, trees and grass. I drop one chukar into the back of my game vest, then another, then climb some more. By the time I climb off the dark mountain in the last light of the day, I have a rare limit of six in the bag and I can see the light of the campfire down by the trailer. When I step into the firelight, Jim is there, smiling. I had gone higher and longer on the mountain than my old friend this day, and I can see the weariness there in him as we laugh. The stories do not come this night, and in the morning, Jim, still game, carries a different gun, a Citori, the Superposed oiled and wiped, standing in the camper closet. By noon, I am again far on the mountain above my friend when I hear his gun bark once, twice. That night, he tells me he killed a double and called it good. Sometimes two birds are enough. More than enough.

***

Now, three autumns after Susan died in her sleep, Jim has pretty much quit carrying the Superposed on any terrain, including ground as level as a Montana pheasant field. I've seen the age on him and sometimes he begs off trips, but I always ask. We pull his trailer east with a pushing October wind and we park it among the ash and boxelders, a tucked-in coulee out of the Montana wind. A third, Greg, has been added to the force, a man younger than me and every bit as interesting, knowledgeable, and affable as my old friend. Greg and Jim hit it off right from the jump, and they talk guns and birds and dogs late into the night. Jim runs through all of his stories and always digs out a few new ones and sometimes it feels as if I'm the crude spectator of a knowledge blizzard that comes from these two. "Can you believe," Jim asks Greg, "that the two of us hunt with a guy who carries an autoloader?"

Greg carries a double 16 mostly, and we walk the prairies and coulees and fell sharptail grouse—one of the West's finest game birds—and rooster pheasants. Sometimes the occasional Hun. It is never the kind of hunting one experiences farther east in the Dakotas. Birds do not just rain out of the sky or pour out of shelterbelts, but there are enough birds to keep a devoted hunter going all day for perhaps a limit of three roosters and four sharptails, but most likely a couple of each. And that is enough. Now in his late 80s, Jim hobbles on old ankles to the end of tree rows, but sometimes he surprises us and walks deep into the CRP, carrying his Citori. The Superposed, if he feels balanced and not dizzy, comes out occasionally.

We have nicknames for the cover on this flung-out Montana ranch. Splashdown is where Jim once felled a rooster from a bluff over a beaver-pond. Top-o-the-world is a wheat field sliced by strings of buffaloberry and old limestone where one can see for miles, all the way into North Dakota. Duke's Turkey Alley is a place where my old bird dog Duke—now gone—pointed a big tom turkey that flushed straight into a barbed wire fence and killed himself. We bought a turkey tag in town and my family enjoyed him for Thanksgiving dinner.

At Bull Pasture, where an old farmstead is surrounded by magnificent tree rows and patches of buffaloberry, on this morning, we see two rooster pheasants on the road duck into a thicket of buffaloberry and rosehip off the road. Jim has been down on his shooting lately, missing the occasional bird from his post position. "I'm feeling weak," he says. But the sight of the birds makes him sit up in the backseat of the pickup.

Maggie is Greg's young setter, a high-energy pup just in her first season. A plan is hatched. Greg will work Maggie on the checkcord until she points. I'll walk in and flush the birds. Jim will push into the field where he can get a good shot before the roosters hit the tree row.

It all goes according to plan. Jim hobbles into position. Maggie makes birds and freezes, her young talent coming to full fruition. I walk in. Up go two rooster pheasants, crossing left to right, together. Even though he had been feeling dizzy and the Superposed is cased and back at camp, Jim swings his Citori and there are two shots—bang, bang—and two rooster pheasants never make it close to the trees. Whoops fill the air, and this is enough to carry Jim smiling all the way home to southwestern Montana and long into winter.

***

Jim is 90 when he mentions that he would like to go hunting up on the Rocky Mountain Front and I jump at the thought. It is an unplanned trip, but one I want, and my wife, Shauna, pushes me to go despite the constant work that is raising little children. A string of days up on the Front with your old friend—that cannot be missed.

We take Jim's outfit, the old trailer—bounced down washboard road from Montana to Baja and points between—with a modest mouse problem from its long storage, and his Ford pickup. I do the driving, gladly. The cooking, the dishwashing, pouring drinks. All of it gladly, gratefully. It feels the least I can do. I get stories and companionship. That is more than enough. I'm doing the hunting too. Jim drives the truck to the end of covers and picks me up, takes me to another cover, then watches my dogs and me out there in it. The Superposed does not even make the trip and his Citori stays cased in the camper closet.

In camp, beneath the skyline that enchanted mountain men and natives on the Old North Trail, that inspired A.B. Guthrie's *The Big Sky*, the aspens are just starting to turn golden. There are sharptail grouse here, at the edge of the mountains, blue grouse on the tall ridges, ruffed in the lush aspen groves. One morning, we drop into a ranch house where Jim knows the occupant well. The old rancher is on a walker and he creaks to his feet, and shakes Jim's hand as one does with old friends seen again. Life, like Montana weather, rolls on. The rancher's wife, too, has passed in the time between Jim's trips up here, and the old widowers shake their heads at the inevitability of time. They talk for a bit about this and that, then we ease back to the pickup truck. I walk fields of snowberry behind my two setter girls and I find grouse. At camp, I step into the aspens and I find grouse. When I step from the cover and walk to camp where Jim is reading a novel in a chair beneath the aspens, his grin is contagious. "Boy am I glad to see you get into some birds. Can you believe that we can hunt grouse right out of camp?"

After days of this, Jim just enjoying the skyline, the sunshine and the aspens, the company and the storytelling, we head home. A half dozen miles from camp, the old camper, on its arthritic axles banged over miles and miles of bad road, gives up the ghost, its back axle cleaving cleanly in half. It is more than forty years old and that, for a travel camper, is the human equivalent of life support. We have no choice but to call a tow truck in far off Shelby and have the camper hauled away. "Well, I think that's the end of that camper. It sure has been fun."

When we get back to Jim's house, I ask him something: "Can I borrow the Superposed? I have some writing I want to do and I want to carry it."

***

Since the beginning of Story, the storytellers have been foiled by the limits. I have no doubt that the chronicler of the hunt, who painstakingly etched the outline of a bighorn sheep into a wall varnished by desert time thousands of years ago, was frustrated by the boundaries of his medium, its limitations and his own. We are all, after all, just vignettes.

"We mortals are but shadows and dust," Oliver Reed's character Proximo told Maximus in the 2000 movie *Gladiator*. Reed, a champion drinker, died in a Malta pub during the filming of the movie after making the mistake of trying to out-drink the British Navy. Shadows and dust indeed; but he left a mark, an etching.

I think about these confines—and about the symbols of our lives and deaths—as I carry the Superposed into the Montana October, hoping to kill just one or two sharptails and thinking, too, of my old friend who was not up to this trip of the uplands. Sharptails are beautiful, wonderful upland game birds that can hold tight for a good bird dog, and my girls do well and the gun swings and connects. I have sat at the campfire of the man who carries this gun for more than thirty years. I have heard how this gun has been taken to the highest mountains after Colorado's ptarmigan, how every fall it made its way in a scabbard aboard a good Fox Trotting horse up a certain mountain outside Crested Butte, Colorado, on a blue grouse expedition. I know its stories too because I have been there and seen it, and what it symbolizes. But these are all just anecdotes, perhaps built out into yarn, expanded into tale, maybe even tome.

There is no way to capture everything that there is about a person in any medium, to capture all that he or she is. Or was. Ron Chernow's weighty biography, *Grant*, tells us much about the President, but it does not tell us his innermost hopes and dreams, doubts and fears. It does not tell us the quiet words he spoke into the ear of his beloved horses, words that only he and the horse knew. The biographer cannot know this and certainly cannot write something long and thorough enough to capture all. No one can, not even Mailer. Uplanders know the brevity of it all better than anyone, for we team with canine and nothing is as fleeting as dog. Cruelly brief, our hearts see-sawed from the joy of a puppy to the tears of an old timer unable to rise from her bed by the fireplace in less time, it seems, than it takes to read this sentence. Then, when we try to tell others about this wonderful animal that blessed us so deeply, we often fall far short of the mark.

He had been having mini-strokes: small episodes that crippled his speech and the right side of his body, then passed. One night a winter or two ago, one had felled him in his living room, and as he waited for it to pass, he thought he should probably just crawl out into the January night and let Montana take him. I understood the sentiment because I understood, just a little bit, the man. I had heard his stories and I had listened and I knew, deep in the meat of those tales was the revealing of his fearlessness, the deep backcountry camps full of drunken armed men who needed to be checked by a solo warden, the cold dark nights on a horse somewhere in thick woods. A harrowing tale of machete-wielding drunk-ass Americans deep in Baja. He had faced it and he would face it, no question.

At the urging of my wife, I had taken on a habit of driving every Friday night around the mountain to see Jim and cook him dinner, drink just a touch of whisky and eat elk or moose or venison tacos. We had shared hundreds of game meat tacos over the years. One night during the meal, another mini-stroke came, and the story he had been telling tailed off into gibberish and he dropped the taco he had been eating. When it passed, he looked at me and told me to never call an ambulance, to just walk away. I looked him in the eye and told him I would, because I understood. I got it. I knew him as well as anyone could know someone. There would be no nursing home, no hospital bed, no special care ward for this man if he could help it.

"The muskrat," wrote H.D. Thoreau, "will gnaw its third leg off to be free." For a few of us—perhaps lucky—how we die can be our last act of freedom. Not long ago, another friend of mine, suffering from a particularly onerous and cruel cancer, took advantage of New Mexico's End of Life Options Act surrounded by his family. *C'est la vie*, say the French—and such is death.

In bitter December, a week after Jim died, I carried the Superposed into a brutal southwestern gale, following my bird dogs, who somehow stepped into the hurricane and pointed coveys of Huns and chukar where Montana meets the Wyoming desert. As I leaned against the wind, I thought about how something as beautiful and functional or ugly and business like as a gun, sometimes fashioned artfully and sometimes crudely, can be a symbol. A symbol of freedom, a symbol of love too. A tool that tells tales, or a tool with one job only. Jim wanted the farm he had worked for under the beautiful Montana sky to pass on to his son, not sold and bled away for medical expenses and "assisted dying."

He wanted the Superposed to be carried by his "other" son.

So I think about this, and about Jim's old dog Pat, on that morning and her partner's next-to-last act, an act of deep kindness for an old dog that might have a full bladder. He propped the front door wide open for her before he sat down with that cheap pistol on the front step.

The birds flushed wild for the most part and caught a tailwind that rocketed them past the wasted strings of shot I sent behind them. A friend who knew Jim was there with me and he had no better luck than I. After two days of this, as the sun started to tip away from our hunt, I convinced Ty to take one more round. For another hour as the Absaroka Mountains squeezed the light away, we pushed into the wind and finally all three dogs—my setters and his griffon—made birds. Up went a covey of Huns in a single burst as Huns are apt to do, and I swung on one male and felled it with Jim's gun: a gun that I will carry for the rest of my life. A gun that will tell stories, if only to me.

Won't You Be My Neighbor
Edgar Castillo

We sat along the shoreline waiting for ducks to fly into a spread of decoys. I was constantly being told to stop jabbering and keep still. This was a difficult thing for a ten-year old boy. Soon afterward, I was banished. My fingers and toes started to regain their feeling in the warm confines of the truck. I stared out the foggy windshield to see small dark shadows appearing. The sound of quacking started coming from the boat. I wiped the glass to see ducks float gently down. They were met by two figures rising with a barrage of gunfire. Seeing the ducks plummet from the gray sky became a scene etched into my soul. It changed my life.

The experiences with my father in the marshes helped form my identity as a bird hunter, just as his experiences laid the foundation for what he would pass on to me. His initiation into hunting has always been mysterious and I knew very little about his hunts besides my own recollections. Recently, I tracked down Tom and he shared his and my father's beginnings. Almost forty years had passed since Tom put my father on the path to become a hunter. They hadn't hunted together in well over three decades.

In the beginning, they were just neighbors, but they became quick hunting partners. One afternoon my father, fueled by his nosiness as to the goings-on and racket of busyness in Tom's garage, walked over to see just what the hell was going on. Tom recalls tinkering with decoys and organizing gear for an upcoming duck hunt. He was sifting through boxes when he heard a heavy Spanish accent say, "What are you doing?" Tom responded that he was going duck hunting, and my father fired off question after question. He wanted to know about the fake ducks, the need for camouflage, and the tiny wooden "whistles." After hours hanging out in the garage, my father said to Tom, "*Señor*, I want to go with you and shoot some *patos*." A week later my father was duck hunting.

Hunting was a new concept to my father. He knew nothing about it. It was the early 1980s and we were still adjusting to the ways of this country. Having come from Guatemala, only the *campesinos* (farmers) hunted. Hunting differed greatly between both countries and culture. In Guatemala, hunting was not a leisure activity, nor a lifestyle, or even a passion.

Hunting was well established in Tom's life. Born and raised in rural South Dakota, Tom would come home from school and toss his school books in the corner, and then leave the house with a shotgun in hand during the autumn months. Tom would walk the equivalent of four blocks, jump a fence (with the permission from the farmer or course) and start hunting. Though young, he was a masterful hunter, and in no time at all he would have a limit of pheasants or a string of ducks.

In 1965, Tom followed his sense of adventure and enlisted in the U.S. Navy. He ended up on an aircraft carrier, preparing jets for bombing runs over Vietnam. After leaving the service, Tom moved to Olathe, Kansas, in the mid-1970s. Years later, Tom found himself sitting next to my father in a duck blind.

Tom knew instantly that a bond had been formed. In the beginning, it was casual, but as the "duck bug" intensified, my father's passion grew. Being neighbors made it easy to sneak off and duck hunt together. The pair primarily hunted the nearby Hillsdale Lake Wildlife Management Area. Their first duck hunt at the lake was in 1982, when construction started on the dam. Tom realized the potential for some good shooting, and scouted the area extensively with my father. They found several waterholes created from excavating, which had filled up with rainwater. With no trees or cover, and only ground vegetation, they set up around the pockets of water and shot ducks as they came in. The location paid off, and my father was rewarded with his first duck: a drake mallard.

Tom filled in the gaps to stories of which I had only heard bits and pieces. I concluded quickly that my father idolized Tom. My father's choice in shotguns and even mannerisms in the field were influenced greatly by Tom. Tom used a 20-gauge Mossberg pump shotgun for ducks. Therefore, my father's first firearm had to be a 20-gauge, just like the *gringo*.

In need of a new toaster and birthday gift for my father, my mother visited the local Sears department store and bought him a 20-gauge Montgomery Wards Western Field pump shotgun for eighty bucks. My mother said she had no idea which *escopeta* (shotgun) to choose. She left the decision to the gentleman working behind the counter. She made it clear that it needed to be a "twenty."

My father even emulated Tom's choice in duck fashion. I remember trying to fit into his stiff, non-insulated rubber waders emblazoned with old-school Marine WWII-style camo. Both wore similar patterned coats to match their "Jones Cap," which was the normal headgear for hunters throughout the 70s and 80s. When not wearing waders, Tom relied on green wool pants to keep him warm, along with his Navy issued heavy wool socks. My father opted to wear "Lectra Sox," which were a brand of gray and red electric socks that ran on 9-volt batteries and kept his little piggies toasty warm.

Tom used a green canvas and brown leather Orvis bag to haul lead-ammo and metal thermoses filled with steaming hot coffee for those blistery mornings in the blind. When not standing in water, they hunted from Tom's fourteen foot V-Bottom Lowe boat. It was propelled by a 25-horsepower Evinrude engine, and a trolling motor to sneak quietly into places. They built a duck blind using gunny sack camo material, which was attached to a PVC and a wooden frame. An empty red 48 oz. Folgers can served as the boat's latrine.

They had a smorgasbord of tales. From watching a 10-foot jon boat overloaded with five hunters and dog capsize, to playing cat-and-mouse with the game warden trying to check them for the waterfowl point system in place at the time. I asked Tom if they ever exceeded their limit.

"Next question," he said.

On the water, three-dozen mallard decoys from the local Kmart were used to fool ducks. Twelve of those were inflatable. Compared to what is hauled out into the duck blind today, Tom and my father hunted with minimal equipment. When the water froze, Tom commandeered his children's yellow sled to pull the decoys across.

Rounding out the gear, each carried only one wooden mallard duck call. Why? Because Tom only used one duck call to lure them in. There were no lanyards rivaling a rapper's delight of duck calls weighing down their necks. Guess how many duck calls I use? One.

Tom felt a good duck hunter only really needed one call. That, however, changed when he read an interesting article in *Field & Stream*. The author wrote about duck hunters employing the use of a squeaky toy to call and attract Pintail ducks. Sprigs were as they are now, a prized duck to shoot. Not scoffing at the idea, Tom went to the local TG&Y store and bought a plastic hamburger squeaky toy.

Within a week, both were sitting in the boat. Tom pulled the toy out and began squeezing it before turning to my father and asking, "What do you think our wives would think about two grown men sitting in a duck boat squeezing a squeaky toy to get ducks?"

No pintail ducks were ever shot while using the squeaky hamburger. However other ducks fell victim to strings of pellets. Was it the squeaky toy that lured them into their demise? Tom doesn't know, either.

Duck hunting led the way to other bird-hunting exploits. My father and Tom soon found themselves chasing the wily rooster and "Gentleman Bob" across Kansas. They enjoyed many years of hunting together. As with all friendships, life inevitably gets in the way.

Tom moved away, and their time afield slowly began to wane, and I became my father's hunting partner, learning the lessons Tom had taught my father. Years passed. Tom became a memory. My father, unable to walk fields, wanted to refocus his hunting priorities back to duck hunting. Though he never really said it to me, I know there was something missing in his life. A void. A friendship.

My father began to retell stories of hunting with Tom, and it was obvious he missed his old friend. In searching for Tom, I was surprised to discover that Tom had moved several times but remained in the area. Tom was more than happy to meet. It was obvious that he, too, missed their friendship and hunting jaunts. Age had caught up with them, but their passion for hunting was still very much alive. I wanted to bring both back together. I concocted a hunter's version of, "Guess who's coming to dinner?" and upon seeing each other, memories and stories began pouring out of both. By the end of the night it was settled, the two were going to get back together and hunt once again.

My father dropped some hard-earned retirement funds into a totally outfitted duck boat instead of a Harley a mere month after renewing their friendship. Something else completely out of character: he ordered a *dozen*, mallard decoys. This is surprising because he has relied on mine—he hadn't owned dekes in almost forty years. He and Tom are now known to wander aimlessly around area outdoor sporting goods stores looking for gear for the boat, and the two have gone duck hunting several times. I've commandeered my friends to help Tom get to easily accessible places to duck hunt due to his bad knees and trouble walking long distances.

They talk about old hunts from their bygone duck boat, and how waterfowl gear has changed. I have since shared several sunrises with both, just as I did when I was a young boy. Tom still ventures into the duck blind wearing the same Jones-style cap he wore four decades ago, and he still uses the worn green and leather canvas bag to carry his ammo. During one such hunt, he quietly produced a lone duck call and began calling. It was obvious to everyone that life was creeping back into Tom's eyes. Hunting had reinvigorated him. There was some new pep in my father, too.

In 2020, Tom shot his fist duck in nearly thirty years—a beautiful drake gadwall. Though he did not shoot it with his 20-gauge Mossberg—it was stolen a long time ago—he dropped the handsome gray duck with a replaced, pristine-condition, 1980s model Browning 12-gauge pump with lustrous wood and an English stock.

Days later, after figuring out how to get Tom into the boat, they found themselves back on the water, anchored twenty feet off a point at Hillsdale Lake. It was the first time the duo had hunted out of a boat in forty years. I watched both shoot a number of species: mallards, goldeneyes, and buffleheads. It was like viewing a rerun, watching both rise out of the camouflaged boat as ducks landed into our decoy spread.

Though there have been many missed shots as well, and difficulties associated with just growing older, a spark had been reignited for both as they clung to their youth to pursue birds. One can easily see it in Tom's eyes, as he's been given an opportunity to reconnect with his love for hunting, and my father. It's evident in my father, too. Though for him it is slightly different, as he knows time is slowly catching up. Tom has provided my father a time capsule of memories and the chance to make new ones.

After each hunt, we rendezvous at a local diner for a cholesterol- and grease-filled breakfast. Duck hunts of years past continue to be retold. As we sip coffee,

Tom is always the first to ask when we are going out again. I love seeing the renewed passion in both, especially my father. The two of them are still teaching me life lessons after all this time. I hope that when I am their age, I, too, will have my best friends around so we can tell stories and make our way into the uplands and marshes.

Tom's mentoring laid the foundation for my father's life, and when it was his turn to mentor me—he succeeded. During our father-and-son duck hunts, he stressed the importance of the hunt, the anticipation, and, more importantly, the lessons learned, and the memories made. But my father was realistic and honest and said that shooting and killing ducks was just as important as the experience.

We cannot choose our neighbors, and we can only hope that a friendship is created and flourishes. Through Tom's mentoring, my father became enthralled by the world of hunting. I am grateful he brought me along with him on his journeys into the marsh—which ultimately led us into the uplands—where we connected as father and son and made our own adventures.

It was my father's and Tom's special bond that led them afield. In turn, bird hunting laid the foundation for my father and I to connect on a profound level. The fields we walked were my classroom. Nature and the outdoors taught me many things about life and death. About balance.

Our relationship grew from our outings. It evolved from a young boy toting a BB-gun wanting to emulate his father, to a man who would many years later carry his father's prized possession into the field: a 12-gauge Ruger Red Label over-under. Years later, as a man, I would find my purpose in the world by committing to a life of serving and protecting for over twenty-six years. Unbeknownst to me, and maybe even my father, our time spent together would provide me with something that would be critical for me years down the road in my profession: peace and tranquility.

The peace I found came from my faith, which in turn helped stabilize the roller coaster of emotions I would encounter as a law enforcement officer and U.S. Marine. The tranquil times afield gave me time to reflect, ponder and treasure. It's been over forty years, but now when I sit hidden in a blind, watching decoys on a cold gray morning, or walking behind a dog across a prairie in search of fluttering wings, I think back to Tom and my father, and the times they shared, and what it brought each of them. I am thankful that they were neighbors. What they passed down onto me without even knowing it would be life-changing.

Greg McReynolds
Solitude

If you hunt uphill, it's always an easy walk home. The strong magnetism of birds and wild places will pull you to the top. Gravity will take you back where you belong.

These wild lands tug at me. I want to be a worthy husband. I want to be a good father. I want my family to float on the buoyancy of my love and attention. But the search for transcendence in a place without people drags me away from these responsibilities. Somewhere out there, the whitewater is roaring, the mountains are calling, the stars are shining brightly under a cold black sky a long way from the lights of men. The wolves are howling, and I yearn to run with them.

We ran with the wolves that became dogs for 40,000 years. We were symbiotic partners roaming the Eurasian steppe, hunting together. Man did not own the wolves; they were volunteers. At some point, we settled down, civilized. Some wolves became dogs and man became something else. We began to fear wolves, and even as we treated dogs more like pets and less like partners, the bond between us remained scratched harshly into our DNA and theirs, with 40,000 years of shared life and death. Dogs and humans gentrified, and wolves remained wild.

Step carefully, watch the dog, mind your pace, one eye on the weather. Meanwhile, wolves range freely across the back of the subconscious. Some synapse ranging around in the deep storage of my brain comes up with a memory from Sunday school thirty-five years gone. Saint Paul taught us, "Harden not your hearts, in the day of temptation in the wilderness." I don't think Paul was writing to the Hebrews about the wilderness that spans the outer edges of the Great Basin, but as I ranged across the basalt and cheatgrass, utterly alone aside from the dog, it occurred to me that maybe he was.

Men aren't supposed to be complicated. Be strong and kind, gentle and tough. Honor your word, don't complain, do good, try hard, lead with generosity, open doors, don't talk down, shake hands, show up, be present, listen, talk less, try to be better. And I don't doubt that men have got the better of it. Since *homo erectus* first leaned into a two-footed trot, men have pretty much done what we want. But people rarely understand things they don't like, and doing what you want and being understood don't always coexist.

The dog understands.

On the last day of chukar season, I stood at the edge of a precipice and thought about falling. The setter stood with me and I wondered what she would do if I fell. She might follow me down, as she had many times before across sketchy scree fields and drops down short, sheer faces. The low winter sun skidded across the horizon while I pondered the long drop and considered how all my actions across my entire life might be summed up in an email to my coworkers. I walked off the hill in the dark with the heavy weight of an empty bird vest.

That night, I woke to a windstorm lashing the canvas of my bedroll. I pulled back the flap to see high, thin clouds racing past the milky way. The smell of sage was strong and good and clean. The snow could come, but not for a while, so I pulled the flap over my head and snuggled into the bag, a soft spot laid over the geologic leavings of a long-dead volcano.

Awake, I thought that I should have gone to sea. The open ocean terrifies, but the self-containment appeals. Not the boat per se, though that is part of it. It is a self-contained team, focused on a singular goal. It is a crew with no-one else to meddle. A true pack. No obstacle besides the ocean itself. I imagine sailing a clipper ship around the Horn and I suspect there is nowhere to hide. We are who we are. We do what we are able. There is no telling, only doing. There is no bluster on the deck of a ship. There is only work and skill and everyone knows.

The world is filled with men who rise with no real idea of how to lead. No particular original thought or ability to see another's viewpoint. It's always the men. When women get to the top, they have earned it. Certain men, though. For some reason they seem to rise; a "who's who" of insider trading or the golden ticket of an Ivy League degree or just the good fortune to be the right guy with a winning smile. Like a cork on the deck of a sinking ship, they bubble up to the surface and reign over us miserable sons-of-bitches who must go down with the ship.

It's an idle thought and I added "sailor" to the long list of failed ambitions.

Just one more thing that I am not and will never be. But I exist to the dog.

In the existential plane of pointing dogs, distance is not measured in straight lines. Birds may run, then hold, or flush, or hold, then run. They might hold at five yards or jump wild at fifty. A dog—some dogs in particular—know the distance. The right dog will push a bird just enough to make it stop running, but not so hard as to make it fly. The cushion between a pointing dog and a given covey or a given bird is unpredictable—except to the dog.

The distance between solitude and loneliness has an unpredictable cushion. We yearn to be alone. We yearn for human connection. We are alone and lonely all at once because to be human is to be many things all at once.

Loneliness is standing next to a person, separated by a vast, dark ocean of unspoken words and forgotten promises. Alone is atop a desolate ridge, miles from the truck, following a dog across the high desert. You mutter to yourself or speak to the dog about birds and the landscape. The wind carries the words away to another place beyond this earthly plane.

The dog is on point, and I break into a lope, swinging wide to try and pin the birds between the setter and I. The dog is perfectly still, but she hears me, smells me, senses my presence. I come into her field of view and I see her eyes watching me. The rest of her is steady. The brilliant white of her fur—surely evolved in recent times—shifts with the wind against the dark hillside. Her nose is high in the air and I know they are further out. She has them on the wind, not hard against the edge. I move out, twenty yards, then thirty and she relocates, right on my heel. A partner, coming in close. They get up going into the wind before swinging to our right. I push the barrels, miss the first shot, and then get myself together and knock one down. We share in the victory. I smooth the feathers while she stands close and drinks in the scent. I slip the bird into my vest and instantly she leaves my side, off again, searching.

Dogs are the archetype volunteers. Some wolf, long ago and likely many times after, decided to pack with humans. The wolves who became dogs chose to stay with us. And now, a dozen millennia on, there are humans who make that same choice.

I imagine my pale, lanky setter would be a poor wolf. I swing my arm in a vague hand signal and watch my white setter loop in a great arc to the south. We have an implied agreement: she goes where I point, I go where she points. It's significant that she even comprehends the gesture at all.

Of all the animals we know, only dogs and elephants will look where you point. Elephants understand pointing and even use it to communicate with each other in ways that we don't fully understand. But otherwise, chimpanzees, gorillas and orangutans can't be taught to look where you gesture. It is a unique skill, critical to our species' success. And somehow, dogs seem to have developed the same skill in conjunction with us. Labradors, pointers, beagles, and Pomeranians, buried somewhere in their DNA, all have the ability to understand pointing.

Even wolves do not easily grasp the concept. It is not a coincidence that dogs understand the significance of pointing. Somehow, intermingled in the genetic cluster that caused some long-ago wolf to choose man, is the ability to literally see the point. Still, I believe it is not merely me that causes the setter to go where I gesture. She goes because some part of her believes in the shared chase and wants us to be successful.

In the thick of it, we are uncontained glee. The birds, the miles, the tired legs. The dogs feel it too, kicking up dust as they run high-speed circles around the truck while I fill water bottles and pockets. We are bound only by our own enthusiasm. We float across the surface of the earth. This is the embodiment of freedom: the ability to wander across an open landscape, uninhibited. Freedom is a funny thing. I hear my neighbors crow about it in my little town. I see them stockpiling and ranting about the government with television talking points and I wonder if they have ever felt the glee of a downhill jog to a dog on point in a truly wild place.

Later, when the season is over, the words that pour onto the page are not the glee of birds and dogs and big wild country, but rather the melancholy of the ending and the longing for a thing that is hard to explain—even to yourself—when seen from outside the moment.

The self-containment of the moment is what makes it so pure, so addictive. Exertion, glee, a point, a rise, a shot. And then we stretch our legs and try again. A beginning and ending—a complete cycle that plays out and begins again. This simplicity is what we yearn for and rarely find in life. Life is inconclusive.

Finality has been replaced by years-long, slow-simmering arguments. We live in an era defined by 24-month contracts, 30-year mortgages and car loans that last longer than it takes to get a PhD. Job tasks stretch on for a decade, and then end abruptly with little fanfare. Until the *final* finale, that is, when we must once more venture on alone.

Alone and lonely are different, but like all things, they can coexist. The wolf and I have run together. We have exerted ourselves, chased and found all that we were looking for, and now we long for the pack. Four rings and then to voicemail. I deserve that and more. A thousand nights, somewhere beyond cell-phone range, out in the wind, I have no right to be disappointed. But I am. Later the call goes through and even after all these years, just hearing her voice gives my heart a flutter.

Over the course of a decade or two, the words get tangled in the actions and the present gets lost in the memories. We are who we are. Age settles on us like shellac. Coat after coat, until our words and actions become a solid, unchanging and impenetrable mass. But even hardened by age, love pulls harder than the wild. I yearn not to be loved, but to show it. The setters are sated. The boots they have worn for the last three days are thrown into the box with collars and empty shot shells and pliers and the detritus of a week living close to the ground. The truck is loaded and pointed for home and my foot grows heavy on the gas pedal. It's late, but if I keep moving, I'll make it near dawn.

This wild and windy space fills my soul. I love my wife as much as the day I married her. The setter understands. Chukar climb. Water rolls to the Pacific. And home is always a downhill run.

T. Edward Nickens
Making Sense

It's different for me. Not better, but neither do I consider mine a lesser experience. Just different, because I don't own a pointing dog, and never have.

Of duck dogs I have had plenty, but never a bird dog. I've hunted quail, woodcock, ruffed grouse, sharptail grouse, pheasant, and ptarmigan, passionately and ardently, and dogless but for the bird dogs of good friends. How to explain my love of bird hunting, when I only bird hunt by tagging along? I've wondered about this. Other modes of dog-based hunting—say, rabbit hunting with hounds—I can take or leave. But a bird hunt is something entirely different. I'll take it every time.

I think it boils down to this: I am not much of a spectator of anything. I don't watch a lot of sports. I want to know that my presence and my decisions impact the outcome. I want skin in the game. And on a bird hunt, even when I'm the proverbial third wheel, I find it. To be sure, the dog owner has more on the line. All that training, and time, and expense adds a gravitas to each moment that isn't on my shoulders, and neither is the sense of reward for all that hard work. Instead, I revel in watching the dogs work, unencumbered by the hopes and expectations that accompany a bird dog owner in the woods.

A memory: in the young woods up ahead, Plexi turns to granite in a tangle of beech saplings. It's been a long morning of nothing, in woods that should be stupid with woodcock, so we can be forgiven for giving the tall, rangy Drahthaar a slight break if she noses up to a nuthatch or sleeping possum. But her body told us that she was convinced, and Plexi's not the sort you want to second-guess. We were sidling toward the point with our heads halfway to the truck when the woodcock went off, twittering towards the North Star and nearly there when Mike fired once to bring it down.

His shot was like calling for a report pair in clay birds: at the shotgun's blast, a cottontail bolted from the beeches in a streak of fur that caught us all off-guard. Plexi, freed from the strictures of holding tight to a bird and fueled by her breeding, spun a 180 and arrowed straight after the bunny. I could barely get the gun up and the trigger pulled while the rabbit was in range, but the shot connected and Plexi plowed into the tumbling bunny like a truck skidding in mud.

How I love that scene: the dog utterly convinced by something I cannot sense—not just a bird, but a rabbit. For Plexi, it must have been a near-overwhelming stew of scent coming from the woods. She lives in a world of sensory input I can only imagine. And it was in that moment that I began to realize what it is about bird-hunting that I find so fascinating. It was months later that I learned there is a word for it.

In 1909, the Baltic-German zoologist Jakob von Uexküll coined a term for a phenomenon that every bird hunter understands intuitively. Von Uexküll noted that every animal exists in its own unique perceptual world—a smorgasbord of sights, smells, sounds and textures that it can sense but that other species might not. The bee isn't attracted to the yellow petals of a sunflower, because it cannot perceive yellow. Instead, it homes in on an ultraviolent target center in the middle of the bloom that the human eye cannot see. We think of taste as an overtly oral act, but other animals do not. Catfish have taste buds all over their bodies. Mosquitoes taste with their feet. These stimuli define what von Uexküll called the *Umwelt*—the world an animal perceives through its own unique senses. The author Ed Yong recently described this in his fascinating book, *An Immense World: How Animal Senses Reveal the Hidden Realms Around Us*, as "an animal's bespoke sliver of reality." That's a description a fine double-gunner could appreciate.

What this means is that we not only experience the world through the glass darkly, but through a glass fractured and smudged. We are walled off from worlds of experience that other animals enjoy (and vice versa, of course.) It's not that a bird dog's sense of smell is simply sharper than a human's. It is so much sharper and wired so differently that it leads to an entirely distinct way of perceiving the world. Dogs have more olfactory receptors and more muzzle real estate devoted to smelling than humans. When a dog exhales, its breath exits through side-facing slits on each side of its nose, which creates tiny tornadoes of scent-laden air that actually draw air back *into* its snout. The act of breathing out is simultaneously the act of breathing in, and a dog can breathe as many as six times per second. Just how sharp a dog's sense of smell is remains up to debate, because we can only imagine such magnitudes. A thousand times sharper than a human's? Ten thousand? What would that even mean?

But every bird hunter has seen the result.

Much of my love for bird hunting springs from this feeling that I am witness to, and a participant in—a richly layered choreography between various ways of experiencing the world. What I see—what I sense—when I'm following a bird dog is only a sliver of what is to be sensed. And while I can't move between and experience these two distinct *Umwelten*—my own and the dog's—I catch glimpses of those hidden realms by watching the dogs at work. It is the next best thing, I suppose, to smelling there.

Another day in the woods, this time with Plexi and Mike, plus Stephen Faust and his cadre of fine Gordon setters. The woodcock aren't everywhere, but a few are around, and we shoulder through creek thickets and cross rocky streams as the dogs seine the woods with purpose. When Blue, one of Faust's Gordons, suddenly slows to a determined stalk along a jumble of privet, river cane, and greenbrier, I watch closely. Blue's flanks pulsate with each inhalation and expiration. His muzzle flares. He searches the ground for the mottled brown bird, but it is his nose that is managing the show. It's the olfactory analogue of flashing red warning signs and yellow signal arrows, the atomized chemical signals detected and sorted and analyzed by the more than 100 million sensory receptor sites in the dog's nasal cavity (humans have about 6 million) and the relatively giant chunk of brain real estate devoted to the sense of smell (about 40 times larger than what exists in a human brain). When Blue locks on point, the setter's eyes turn flinty and focused. The *Umwelten* collide.

I move toward the unmoving Blue, and micro-manage my position. Knowing what is to come, I edit my own reality—my own location in this space and how I can fine-tune the sensory inputs to take advantage of a bird flushing. I take two steps to the left so the shadow of a tall pine shades my eyes. A half-stop back to move off a downed branch and settle my boots for solid footing. I snap off a branch that might bump the shotgun barrel. This is how I bring myself to the game. This is one of the beauties of woodcocking, this thoughtful, intimate arrangement, a purposeful *mise-on-scène* in that moment before the dog is released and the bird flies.

"I'm good," I say, and Faust sends Blue forward. When the woodcock flushes,

I mount the shotgun and swing. What happens in the next moment matters, whether or not it leads to fluffs of feathers snagged in the beech twigs and a happy muzzle full of bird. But it can't compare to the moment before the rush and the flush and the push on the shoulder and the crisp tang of cordite in the nostrils. That moment of encounter, of closing the circle with a wild fragment from a faraway place, led by a nose that senses what I can but meagerly imagine.

And then, suddenly, as is often the case with the timberdoodle, the birds are everywhere. The ground is splattered with chalk. "Look at all this splash," Faust says. "For those dogs, this must be like walking through a bakery."

Or a butcher shop. Or a landfill, even. When Blue brings the bird to hand it is another telling reminder that the world I know is only a sliver of the world that is to be known. And for those fleeting days of fall and the flinty days of winter, a bird dog is my only guide to the unseen domains that I've only begun to explore.

Shauna Stephenson
What's Left of Lolo

In the depths of the upright freezer, just beyond the frozen tamales and next to the shredded zucchini, is a folded paper grocery bag containing the body of Lolo.

What's left of Lolo.

In likelihood—in the natural process of grief, or what your average therapist might categorize as natural—she's been in there too long, resting between the carrots we put in there two winters ago, the asparagus we plucked from the garden the following spring, the pie cherries we harvested from our tree in the depth of summer.

I don't think of her much anymore, nor does it give me a feeling of sadness to shuffle her around to make space for the groceries that must come in and out of any farm kitchen and pantry. She is just part of what remains frozen.

When we found her, half of her breast had been eaten—a meal for a hungry owl or eagle. To the falcon, to the owl, to the eagle, death is simply part of being. Most of your day is spent trying to be the one doing it, not the one it is done to.

The upland crowd often laments the short life-season of the dog. But most have never known the falcon. The falcon knows unequivocally that death is the most natural part of life.

Falcons have evolved enough to accept this, if acceptance is indeed an animal trait. Live in the moment and then move on.

Humans aren't there yet.

We keep a flock of pigeons next to the dog kennel on the farm. Technically, they're probably homing pigeons, but after too many decided to take up residence in the shed, crapping on the truck instead of returning to their nests, their homing privileges were revoked.

"Pigeons are nothing but herpes-infested, filthy, flying rats."

Scott, my falconry sponsor, was a dirt hawker with a few longwings in his past. He didn't mess with pigeons. Dirt hawkers are falconers who fly shorter-winged birds who hunt with bursts of speed instead of relying on aerodynamics and gravity to rocket them toward their prey. They lean toward goshawks, red-tailed hawks, eagles—birds that didn't need pigeons to chase to get into shape for hunting season.

A master falconer, Scott could tell you every way to mess up a bird, all from experience. And the thing about Scott is, he was never afraid to tell you.

"Why in God's name would you get a rat?" he said as I opened the flap on the brown "live animal" box. I had my newly printed apprentice license, and it was our first day trapping. Hawk trapping was simply driving up and down country highways looking for a hawk gullible enough to land on a wire trap covered in slip knots.

"Didn't I say, get a hamster?"

"But I could get two rats for the price of one hamster."

"Do you really think now is the time to be thrifty?"

"But rats and mice are their natural…"

"Oh I know, I know, I know…"

He sucked his bottom lip into the gap in his lower teeth with a popping noise. A southerner by birth, he had a way of dropping his drawl an octave when he felt his audience was particularly dense.

The tradition of training new practitioners in falconry is a long and tenuous thread. Ancient knowledge handed down from master to apprentice. Even today, a new falconer must come under the tutelage of a seasoned hunter before their license will be granted. Some take this seriously. Others do not. The good ones, like Scott, take it as a personal calling.

"Look," he said, "Rats are smart. Hamsters are stupid. When a rat spots a raptor, they freeze. A hamster is too dumb to know any better and will waddle around in that trap until the hawk can't stand it. That's why I told you to get a damn hamster."

"They made me sign a form saying I would treat my animal kindly."

"Oh hell, you're not hurting them. They're doing a job. They waddle around, get the piss scared out of them by a hawk and if they don't have a heart attack on the spot, they get to retire to a life of hamster leisure."

Advice from Scott was always like reaching blindfolded into a sack full of cats. Sometimes you got something loud and feral, but every now and then there would be a gem.

"There's falconers out there who think they're great because they take a limit of huns or ducks. They think because they can throw enough money at the sport or have the most expensive, best-bred birds, that they walk on water. But at the end of the day, they toss those birds back in the mews like hanging up a gun. And they don't think about them again."

He shook his head in dismay.

"It's the ones who took the time to build that relationship with the bird—they are the great ones. People think they're wild animals, and they may be. They think you can just throw them back in the mews and walk away. But they're missing the point. They're missing all of it. When we can make that connection with a wild animal, start seeing what they see and start hearing what they hear, that's when we start understanding the world around us."

***

In the history of mankind there have been three species we have learned to partner with—that is, we work together toward a mutually beneficial goal. The dog has always been a given, churning out generations of "man's best friend" relationships. And it makes sense. Who doesn't prefer a partner who wags their tail every time they enter a room, emitting an endless shower of wordless affection?

Those who prefer a less needy partner often turn to horses. Sure, some limited affection is nice, but the working relationship doesn't necessarily suffer if your capacity for emotional giving is slightly stunted. They don't wilt from an uttered curse or tuck their tail and pout if you look at them wrong.

The falcon is a different sort of relationship. From a purely unemotional standpoint, you could probably throw it into the category of a very high-maintenance tool. A weapon requiring its own special diet, facilities, care, and maintenance.

But if you're willing to peel back that layer and talk about the true relationship between man and bird of prey, you'll find a whole next level of potential fodder for the therapist.

True, they tend to be weirdos. It is only the falcon that we could not quite tame—the one who learned to train us to their advantage, rather than them to ours.

For the falcon it means a cushy home, regular food, a human to serve them.

For the falconer it's a life that revolves around feeding and weighing and watching the weather and wind speed, training and continually feeding a flock of herpes-infested, filthy, flying rats.

But what is it also? Something otherworldly, that goes beyond a line we arbitrarily define and falls into that category of "I felt it but I can't name it." Just a little woo-woo for the world of upland sport.

***

And so we arrive at the basics of falconry, in a brief and unscientific summation:

Find a sponsor and get the licenses. And there are lots. Hoop after bureaucratic hoop: facilities to be inspected, tests to pass. State, federal. All of it. If you think it's something you'll just take up as a part time hobby like sourdough bread baking or knitting, you might as well forget it. Those first few years are intense.

The fine print behind you, you can now get the bird. Some trap their bird using elaborate homemade contraptions; some scale cliffs and trees to pull an extra fledgling from a nest (there are very strict rules and traditions on this). Some purchase a bird from a breeder. Each have their own circumstances, pros, cons and level of skill.

Now, bird in hand, you train. Not like a dog with your "No! Don't pee on the carpet." A falcon could care less about your "No!" and would just as happily bite the shit out of you if you think you're going to tell them what they will and won't do.

This is positive association 101. Train it to trust you. Train it to know that you are the food wagon. Train it to tap into your body language, all the while being 10 steps ahead of theirs. For every one thing you do, there are 15 things you better not, or you'll have a leg ripping monster on your hands. Think. Think. Overthink. Every single interaction.

Then, mess it all up. You will. Mess it up and then start all over. Beg forgiveness of your bird and hope to heck those puncture wounds don't get infected.

Build that relationship. Think about what they're thinking about. See what they are seeing. Hear what they are hearing. This is the most important part.

At some point you'll know it's time to fly. Don't dilly dally. Think, think, overthink. And then just do it. Go for it. Remove the leash, slip on the flying jesses, pull the hood and let them go, knowing it could go one of two ways. Either they come back, or they keep going.

Either way you will never feel...*So. Fucking. Free.*

***

The masters of the art are otherworldly. Some ride fast-moving horses, bird perched on their non-dominant hand, looking out on their hunting dogs as they work the ground ahead of them. Longwingers, they are called, and their craft is as ancient as that of the general on the battlefield.

The dogs point, the hood comes off and the falcon climbs, watching the dogs from its position in the sky. The signal is given to flush and the falcon stoops onto its prey. From its position in the sky. The signal is given to flush and the falcon stoops onto its prey, knocking it from its position in the sky in an explosion of feathers.

On the ground, they break into their prize, bird dogs laying at their side to protect them until the master arrives. It's a dance where every step must be just right. If someone doesn't do their part, the whole thing unravels. The horse must not flinch. The dog must stand steady. The bird must trust the army behind it.

Others—dirt-hawkers—carry red-eyed goshawks or toddler sized golden eagles on their gloves as they work sagebrush for cottontails and jackrabbits. The dog points, the bird leaps from the glove and takes off in an explosion of acrobatic speed, single-mindedly pursuing its prey in a way that is just…otherworldly.

***

Is it silly to believe we are not finite? The edges of ourselves do not end at the tips of our fingers and toes. Our senses expand beyond five. Our connection to the world around us can be less scientific and more guttural and instinctual. We are not "just animals," bumbling around on this earth. At our best, we can be as amazing as animals.

I was listening to a lecture on the microbiology of soil the other day when the speaker made the point that just because our culture doesn't necessarily believe we can communicate with nature, and that nature can communicate with us, doesn't make it true.

"If nine of ten cultures in the world believe we can talk to the plants and animals, then what becomes of the one that does not?" he asked. "In science, the data point that doesn't fit the set is thrown out. It's an outlier."

Lolo came from a breeder in Utah. A pretty little brown and white peregrine falcon crossed with gyrfalcon, she was bred for speed and size, for taking down the larger upland birds in the West. As a juvenile, she was still learning the limits of her own wings, and we spent a season learning together, chasing pigeons, walking fields, learning to work with the dog.

We became better acquainted with the intricacies of our own backyard. The pair of crows that lived in the field down by the railroad track. The sandhill crane who decided to overwinter with the neighbor's steers. The Swainson's hawk who hunted off the three same telephone poles every single day. Things that passed us by every other day, but now had a place and a home and a reason.

See the things they see. Hear the things they hear. Think, think, and then overthink.

She spent the winter on our dining room table, greeting us as we walked in the door, watching the kids as they did crafts, taunting the cat as she skulked through the room.

By the second season, her plumage had turned slatey gray, her breast a soft cream and her long, delicate feet bright yellow. She was an adult, ready to hunt ,and we spent the fall and first part of the winter chasing birds, but never with any tangible success.

Worried she wasn't climbing high enough to get a fast enough stoop, I began to focus more on training her to gain altitude more immediately. I saw other falconers' success in the field and felt the pressure of my own ambition. It was nearing the end of the winter and spring winds had started to blow. To train falcons to climb, a kite, or nowadays, a drone, is put up in the air with a reward dangling below. The birds climb, grab the reward which detaches, and then return to the ground to eat.

In this case, it was a giant rainbow kite with a dead quail dangling about 15 feet below. A cold wind had picked up and Lolo sat on my foot with her hood on as I let line out, watching the kite and quail drift higher. Once the kite was in position,

I reached down to remove Lolo's hood.

I probably should have listened. Either to her, or to that extra sense. The one that said, *Today isn't the day. It's too windy. The eagles and owls are too hungry. You're taking a chance.* But my less evolved self was louder. *Your bird isn't progressing fast enough. She's not performing. You're not driven enough.*

Lolo roused in the wind, fluffing her feathers and then looked up at me, hesitating. Maybe she was questioning the wind speed. Maybe she saw the eyes of the predators already around us, hiding in the cottonwoods and willows. But it wasn't enough. She saw the dead quail and was airborne, ringing up, pumping her wings to cut through the wind and climb to her reward.

A gust of wind came through the valley as she reached the dangling body. The kite snapped. Her wings caught the gust and, quail in hand, she was blown off course, veering toward the willows like a pilot who has lost control.

We found her under a willow the next day, or rather, the dogs did. Her slate-gray wings were tucked under her, her eyes closed. The meat on her breast had been eaten away. There was no sign of the quail.

In my haste to be a human, I forgot we were both animals and animals don't recognize ambition.

"Cry," says Scott. "Cry and grieve and feel awful. Beat yourself up. Learn something. And then move on. Start over. It's how the natural world works."

***

Now there is Bonnie, a large female prairie falcon. She's a mean little thing and spent most of her first year here trying to disembowel me. Prairies are notoriously fierce creatures. Taken from a nest in the Bonneville basin, she came to me in her later years at the age of 10 on the very first day of pandemic lockdown.

She has mellowed in the years she has been here. Now she sits with me in the greenhouse as I pot up fennel for the hoop house, alternating between screaming and playfully nipping my gloved fingers, wanting to be picked up.

We don't go out as much as I'd like. Kids, a farm and adult responsibilities tend to eat up the time that was once my own. But every now and then we grab a pigeon and go play in the air currents, zooming across the pasture and buzzing the tops of the old cottonwood trees.

The winter has been harsh. The Swainson's hawk still frequents the same three telephone poles, although he's been tucking in somewhere I have yet to find when storms roll through. The sandhill crane has been out on the feed line with the steers but I haven't seen the crows.

One of these days the snow will clear and a warm patch of ground will open up. I'll tuck a dead quail into a pocket, hood Bonnie and grab the paper bag from the freezer and we'll hike to the upper pasture where the sagebrush rolls on forever before running into the stone wall of the mountains. The natural world is awash in contradiction.

Pulling her hood, I'll send her out, watching her fly. I don't care how fast she climbs anymore. Or how she hunts. It's enough to simply be there, to feel the sun and hear old friends in the trees, to see her joy in the freedom of flight. To be present in all the ways I can be. It's a state of mind I've learned in the years since Lolo, and for humans it takes some work to get to.

Once there, I can finally unwrap the paper bag and return Lolo—what's left of Lolo—to the earth, gazing up into the blue that goes on and on, far beyond the edges we see until we let go and tip into the forever we can only begin to sense.

Chris Dombrowski
Christmas Eve

If there's a finer pleasure in wing-shooting than cresting a hill and, after scanning the windblown contours of the country, finding your dog buried on coal-hot covey point amongst riffling clumps of bunch grass and the rattling leaves of dry balsamroot, please inform me of its whereabouts.

Our Llewellin setter Zeke gave me just such a point yesterday. I say "gave" not because he owes me a penny, but because if I were to look under the Christmas tree tomorrow and unwrap a box somehow containing that likeness—black mask unflinching, frame as tight as a drawn bow-string—I would not need or want another present. He was low and he was staunch. He'd been there for a while, at least a couple of minutes. I could tell by the direction of his gaze that the birds were in front of him, down the south-facing hill from us. I took a few steps past him and, watching him steady in the corner of my eye, did something I rarely do before pointed birds flush: clicked the Browning's safety off.

On my next footfall, fifteen Huns flushed downhill and I picked one from the left side of the winged chaos and dropped it, then tried for a late right-swinging double and missed. As Zeke brought the dead bird back to me, I praised him for his brilliance. I drew the warm creature from his jaws, smelled its mottled cape in feral ritual, and silently pledged to extend its life in a savored meal. Then I sighed deeply and considered my good fortune to be alive and afield at all.

My hunting partner Mahoney, his ten-month-old Lewellin female Olive, and our old friend Beaver Shocker strode over the hill to see how I'd done. We'd brought along Shocker not for his nickname—earned, I assure you, during his days as a fisheries tech with Montana Fish, Wildlife and Parks—but for his reliable gunning, so that we could, while Shocker walked up the coveys, capture more photos than our nerves would normally allow for. While I relish solo hunts, company can aid high-country Hun pursuit: another pair of legs to push you up the ridge-spine; another conscience to remind you that limit chasing likely limits next year's yield; another student of maps occasionally inclined to share a very birdy tract of land he's found.

Discovered by Mahoney late last season, the roughly 4,000-acre mid-elevation grassland bowl we plied yesterday is comprised of three unforested mountainsides, each of which features numerous nobs of sand-colored cheatgrass and long, gently-sloped saddles. Flanking the hills, perfect harsh weather habitat for birds, three creek drainages stitched with hawthorns and rosehips fall into a sage-choked basin. Though we have found only grasshoppers and green sprouted cheat in the crops of birds harvested here, winter forage of snow- and grouse-berries abounds in the gullies, as do the tracks of mule deer, elk, coyote, black bear, and wolf.

***

After a decade of dedicated pheasant hunting, I fell hard for Huns this fall, much the way I fell for French wines: not because I was supposed to, but because they are superior in nuance and challenge.

In his sixth season, Zeke has appeared to relish the change in terrain dictated by our new quarry, the parceled agricultural acreages frequented by pheasants replaced with the seemingly interminable, non-linear grasslands in which Huns thrive. If his GPS tracker is accurate, Zeke routinely logs upwards of thirty-five miles per hunt, most covered at a loping gait, while wearing a gluttonous grin, until the unassailable scent of a hard-won covey seizes him and his brow furrows with focus. As Zeke's understanding of the species has evolved, I have, I believe, evolved as a trainer. In both child rearing and dog-handling, the Third Newtonian Principle of Motion applies: genetic predispositions aside, most of Zeke's "less than desirable" habits and tendencies can likely be attributed to my early flailing as a dog-dad and shotgunner. To wit, I have tried this season to focus on his reactions to his environment, to understanding his decisions as a part of his growing comprehension, rather than the mere lead-up to my shooting opportunities. On our best hunts, I have spewed fewer directions and commands than in the past—though we did engage in one very frank discussion several weeks ago. More on that soon.

The vital exchanges, of course, have taken place between dog and bird, Zeke's two hundred and twenty million scent receptors conversing with the birds' nuanced redolence and tendencies; his pursuit genes talking with their *de rigueur* caginess; his instincts squaring off in debate against theirs. While we experienced successful outings for Huns last year, what evaded me—both because he efficiently located many coveys, and because adrenaline compromises observation—was that the slow striding "pheasant creep" he often employs successfully on cagy roosters forced some coveys to wild flush.

When Zeke exhibited such behavior in early November, though, I perked up.

By the last few inches of his white tail, I had located him in a robust expanse of sage, and walked a hundred paces to his staunch, lip-quivering lockdown. But when I reached him and the covey scurried visibly through dry understory, he reset with panic, abandoning point too quickly, too wildly, to be whoa-ed. The birds flushed—a huge covey swirling like a colony of bees—but I didn't mount my gun. Immediately, I called him in from his quasi-victory lap and said: "No way. No way that is going to work for us." He sat beside me panting, improbably long tongue dangling from his mouth, looking preoccupied if a tad bit annoyed, ready to cut the next scent. In the past I might have barked something else in frustration, but I had a hunch that he required a longer leash to learn this new bird on his own. So I got down on both knees, pulled his face to mine and, in the manner of a desperate supplicant, pleaded.

"You have to understand, you keep making that move, these birds will bust every time. Every time. You will never get a mouthful of feathers."

It struck me that swapping targets—fleet, cocky, stop-and-go pheasants that will run until pinned, for eggshell-fragile coveys of Huns that will hold tight for days unless bumped—was a lot to ask of an experienced, damned good rooster dog. I picked a handful of sage from a branch and, crumbling the leaves in my gloved hand, began to ponder our situation. Awakened by the scent, I reasoned that the only way to help Zeke with the transition was to spend far more time in Hun country; twist my shooting arm, it was a sacrifice I'd have to make. So we committed to our course of study and, except for a few moments of backsliding, Zeke has seemed to comprehend my monologue verbatim.

***

If I ever cease to marvel at how a domesticated canine with a nose the size of a cracker can manage to scent, amidst a square-mile plain of grasses, a dozen wild game birds that huddled together would barely cover a serving plate, I hope a hunting partner has the good sense to confiscate my shotgun from me for a week in mid-November. After the dogs nailed the second covey, we praised their feat effusively, watered them, and gradually began to talk strategy, soon deducing that we'd found both groups of birds at similar elevation. Mahoney hedged that our most productive method of chase might simply be to side-hill around the vast parcel of public land, to cut a line around the inside of the bowl rather than over its lip; following this directional aim, the dogs over the next four hours located thirteen more coveys, only three of which were "re-finds." Still in her first season, the lanky, blue-eyed Olive had a breakout day, sticking six coveys solo, retrieving birds to hand, and backing on sight. With a high, thorough nose, Zeke quartered wide, approached coveys deftly, and stood them for long spans of time. To speak it plainly, the more ground we covered, the more birds we found, our Hun equation solved—per the Kierkegaard adage, *solvitur ambulando*—by walking.

We didn't have to walk far, though, on the third mountain, before Zeke downshifted, picked up his nose, and yard-by-yard disappeared over a rise. Shocker and I followed and a few minutes later, after crossing a cattle-hammered sage plain, found him sky-lined, leaning into a point. I turned on the phone's video recorder and pushed Shocker forward into my view screen. Zeke tiptoed two steps; I "whoa-ed" him softly. Then Shocker stepped past the point, crossed an invisible threshold and flushed the covey, firing his old wood-stocked .870 once when the covey reached its apex. The bird over his right shoulder flipped and tumbled hard. I marked it through the view screen, but when I walked to where the bird had fallen, I found only Shocker's shot-shell wad.

Like a couple of forensics investigators, we retraced our steps and tried to locate the downed bird in slow-motion video replay, while Zeke repeatedly attempted to cast downhill, each time ceding to my calls of, "Here, hunt dead." Shocker seemed to want to concede—it didn't help that Mahoney and Olive had, from the sounds of things, found a covey and some shooting—but I'd watched the bird plummet too heavy to abandon the chase. After another several minutes Shocker even asked, innocently enough, whether we would be better served with a Lab that was good on cripples. Fearing I'd jinx our search but desperately needing to defend my dog's honor, I told him that, though it seemed unlikely given the circumstances, Zeke hadn't lost a bird all year. I knocked on my gunstock for luck. Shortly thereafter, in the swale he'd wanted to search before I'd called him to obey my inclination, Zeke went on loose point—tail parallel to the ground, rear haunches loose—with the still-live bird directly under his nose. The essence of steppe-reared grit, the umber-crowned bird was dispatched fifty yards downhill from where it had first fallen.

By the time we reached Mahoney in the next basin north, we all carried "So, here's the story" smiles, but before we could swap tales, Zeke and a backing Olive tightened into points up the slope from us. On camera duty, I was stupidly talking loudly—ushering Jeff toward the shot, assuring him that I wanted to film—and thus the covey of twenty flushed at the edge of range. Nonetheless, Mahoney dumped a late-rising single; Zeke trailed its descent, but Olive came in hot, thirty-five pounds of tricolored blur, and the gentleman swung off. I marked the covey's disappearance over a steep rise to the east, and we banked west to give the birds time to settle and throw scent.

Almost too quickly, the dogs were slowed by another scent cone, with age backing youth this time. Again we fumbled with our roles on the large covey rise, dropping phones to shoulder guns, and fanned—three up, three down—but marked the well-lit birds up the canyon, in the vicinity of the aforementioned group. More giddy than chagrined, liberally approximating the numbers now collected in the draw, we worked our way toward a pinch of cliffs that seemed to harbor, the way an attic would, a palpable level of hiddenness. Lost in modest reverie, I reckoned that no two-legged traveler had traversed the location for quite a while and, reaching the rim, followed Zeke downhill, to my right, despite having seen both groups of birds banking unmistakably left.

I chalked up the acquiescence to "trusting my dog," and looked toward Mahoney.

He was already shooting me a glance, a silent query: *Want us to wait?*

I shrugged an indecisive, equally silent response and strode toward my dog.

You should call Zeke and work up the drainage with them, a voice in my head soon told me. Zeke had crested the next hill, though, and I didn't want to call him off a would-be scent. A few minutes later shotgun reports caromed off the rock wall—two shots from two distinct guns, and not long after, two more—and a recognizable voice intoned: *I told you so.*

I could see the truck in the distance on the valley floor, and let gravity have its way with my spent frame. After a while, still a good ways from the two-track, I sat down and called Zeke to my side to water him. He drank sloppily from his Tupperware dish, and then slumped down, a puppet abandoned by its master's hands, head in my lap.

"What a good boy you are," I said, while scratching him behind the ears. Near his tired wagging tail, atop a slab of ochre fieldstone specked with ancient lichen, lay the caterpillar-curled, white-tipped dropping of a Hun. "You have been absolutely killing it on these Huns. Are you having fun with them? Are you? Thank you, buddy."

***

Not long after the novelist David Foster Wallace took his own life, Jim Harrison, who corresponded with Wallace and endured many of his own battles with depression, lamented in an interview: "Of the twelve or thirteen suicides I've known, none of them had any interest in nature. They couldn't make that jump out of themselves." Not condescending, not casting a single iota of blame, but rather speaking from the primacy of immediate experience, Harrison speculated that Wallace might have fared better had he spent more time with dogs. "You know, Wallace loved his dogs for that last year, but he should have been having dogs for thirty years. I absolutely depend on them."

If only because the hackneyed image of the emotionally impenetrable Great White Hunter is as useful as the Marlboro Man's left lung, I'll come forward with this confession: psychologically, emotionally, I barely survived last winter.

Perhaps while logging ten-hour days at the desk, delving old traumas in a new manuscript, I wrote my way into the deep depression that overtook me mid-January. I certainly didn't drink myself there, as I'd given up my nightly two-glass dose of wine early in the flu season in hopes of bolstering my immune system. Serious illness gripped our community—the mother of a student at our daughters' school, where Mary teaches, died of the flu—and our family's proximity to the lethal virus fed my anxiety. Unlike past plunges into what Kierkegaard rightly called "the netherworld," this mental disequilibrium didn't appear to be seasonally or circumstantially induced; I had regular doses of fresh air, some money in the bank, and meaningful work to go to each day.

But daily, I failed to find footing in the ill-lit warrens of my mind.

One afternoon, I found myself sitting alone in a back pew at Saint Francis Xavier, a place I visit often when it's vacant so that I can admire the elaborate frescoes painted in the late-1800s by a Jesuit kitchen worker, an Italian transplant to Montana. Threadbare, all but undone, I scanned the Stations and the well-known Gospel scenes until an image of Francis himself—robed, lightly haloed, reclining with eyes closed, perhaps napping, a tamed wolf lying in the dirt at his side—focalized my gaze. The room was still save a single flickering votive near the entryway, and I recalled a candle that Joyce Bahle, Harrison's long-trusted assistant, had lit here while Jim's health was failing.

"Do you know of any quiet chapels in town," she'd asked without pretext, almost frantically, during our somber lunch at a Missoula cafe. "I have this urge to light a candle. I haven't been in a church since childhood."

Thinking of the mysterious urgency of Joyce's gesture in the same alcove, I remembered a line of Jim's—"We are here to be curious, not consoled"—from a poem he once described as "a record of deliverance, which is always near but often quite invisible." The words hit me like a load of bismuth #5s. "Invisible" implied existent, within the realm of possibility, which at the moment seemed irreconcilably far-fetched. I was pouring every ounce of energy and positivity that I could muster into transcending my moment-to-moment disrepair, to pitiful results.

***

Back on the mountain with Zeke yesterday, I felt enough distance from last winter's mental anguish to look it in the eye, and hold point. As ever, I was superstitious, knocking on my gunstock again. I didn't want to outrun my nose, per se, but wondered why, given last winter's emotional stranglehold, the coming winter months weren't a constant source of preoccupation? Perhaps because my dog—behind his nose and hunches and indefatigable drive—had led me into so many luminous moments of late. I felt as if I carried by shoulder strap a cache of twilit white tails on point, light enough to see me through the dark—and it struck me, with my hand in his coat, that I was thanking Zeke for far more than finding birds.

"To feel most beautifully alive," Gaston Bachelard said, "means to be reading something beautiful."

All autumn I had been immersed in it—the first and most vital text, this terrestrial earth and its creatures—with Zeke as my primary translator. I had made countless entries and notations in the field journal of the mind, and possessed, because of Zeke, sufficient glow by which to read them. It's an old story. The season nears its brutal close and the hunter reaches back into his game-pouch for something more than bird.
"Your body," a wise friend recently told me, "is how the land thinks itself into you, and vice versa."
As Zeke began to stir, I comprehended something new: when the land isn't thinking itself into me, I'm thinking *myself* into me—an abysmal trade.

Without warning then, a thermal slid down the mountain and Zeke picked up his nose from my lap. The wind had changed and he rose and cast elastically, with extreme caution, into a small bowl on the south-facing slope. Gradually, not more than a couple hundred yards from where we'd been loafing, he fell into a stymied sort of point. He was steady, but facing downhill toward ground he'd just covered. I puzzled over his stance, but stood and loaded two shells and closed the over-under. Very slowly then, like the minute hand of the clock I tracked in elementary school before each bell, his nose dialed around to the north and his tail rose with assurance.

There were birds not far off his nose, a tight braid of at least fifteen that flushed down-light. I felled one from the back of the group and aged it over a few days in the cool garage and cooked it simply in salt and pepper, and olive oil, with a glaze of homemade chutney. I served it centerpiece atop a bed of sautéed kale, mushrooms, and cayenne beet slices, and washed it all down with a barnyardy red blend from Catalans.

But for now, gentle reader, I prefer to leave Zeke where he was: lordly, motionless as a fold in the landscape, at the precise moment of the covey rise, when the hunter's heart tries to leap from its cage.

And the hunter leaps out of himself, as his dog taught him to.
Christmas Eve *first appeared in Gray's Sporting Journal.*

Els Van Woert
Connection

Prologue

Early in our relationship, my college boyfriend, Simon, rushed home to be with his dying family dog, a black Lab named Alis. For one last outing, Simon paddled Alis around in a canoe, chasing geese off the water as her ears perked up. After the vet put her down, Simon helped lower Alis into her grave, burying with her memorabilia from her life and his childhood.

Back then, Simon's parents were splitting up and his car bore a bumper sticker that read "the more people I meet, the more I like my dog." I wasn't sure if it resonated with him because of his love of dogs or due to reticence about people. But I imagined that when Simon buried Alis, some sense of family went with her, a loss that I hoped might be repaired in time. Simon's devotion amid mourning spoke to me of his character. I noticed how, in Alis' final hours, he centered her heart's desire, which was to be with her people and chase birds.

Simon shared that, in her heyday, Alis birthed a litter of puppies, accidentally sired by his family's English pointer. As Alis showed signs of early labor, Simon volunteered to keep watch overnight. Waking up to a puppy being born, he roused his parents. It was an experience that left a mark. My mom bred chocolate Labs in my childhood, so my sense of the world was also shaped by puppies, most of all their fierce and attentive love as they chased four-year-old me across our grassy yard.

While I shared a love of dogs with Simon, we came to it differently. My family hiked mountains with our dogs. My parents saw the great outdoors as a spiritual refuge, the way in through scenic beauty atop peaks, and they imparted to me an ecological ethos of "do no harm." Simon grew up with dogs as partners in the field, helping train them to scent and retrieve grouse and other game birds. His was a sporting life rooted in conservation-minded fair chase, replete with heirlooms such as his great-grandmother's shotgun and outdoor opportunities arising from the family business, Orvis.

When I met Simon in college, he prioritized wood-chucking in the Vermont wildlands alongside, if not above, his studies. The passion Simon held for these hobbies, while foreign to me, was part of his intrigue. I admired his self-trust about what he loved; especially so, as I sought to more fully understand my own place in the world and what felt truest to me.

Copa

After college, Simon and I moved into a tan ranch house in Helena, Montana. I interned at an environmental nonprofit and Simon guided fly-fishing trips. A month after we moved, Simon spent three focused hours at a breeder picking out the first dog that would truly be his, a small tricolor English setter, predominantly white with asymmetrical face markings and a big black dot on her back. I liked how her step was springy as she played with the other puppies.

Simon named her Copa, and soon landed a gig as a guide-in-training at a remote upland bird hunting lodge on the prairie of north-central Montana. As he shared that he planned to spend the fall with Copa two hours away, I thought, *Wait. Hadn't the plan been to live together?*

I felt startled, left behind. Wondering where he was going and what upland hunting was all about, I oscillated between self-righteous judgment at the seeming machismo bloodthirst of it and curiosity about what was so powerfully calling to Simon. Through the fall, Simon called most nights, driving from the lodge to a specific spot where he got cell service to check in. Even so, I felt like an outsider. We grew distant, and by the end of hunting season, we broke up and I moved out.

The Training Hunt

After months apart, however, Simon and I reunited and I moved back in. We worked to repair our differences, Simon trying to invite me into his world more, and me trying to be more self-sufficient in my passions while staying open to his.

By the time the next upland season rolled around, Simon got promoted to full-time guide, a dream he'd had for as long as he could remember. To get the canine power he needed for his job, Simon borrowed dogs from family members, promising to train them up in exchange. The dogs arrived that August in the days leading up to the season opener. There were English setters, English pointers and

Labs, as many as eight per season. Some dogs came by car, others on airplanes. Each time a dog flew in, we drove across town to the regional airport to pick them up. They whapped their tails, tap danced, and howled playfully at us as we greeted them.

I took the dogs along with me on trail runs to prepare them for covering miles of ground. Simon also needed to get them in front of birds to make sure their skills were sharp. One August day, a friend welcomed us to walk the open field behind his house a few miles out of town to see what the dogs could find. Though Simon had described the mechanics of bird hunting to me, I hadn't yet witnessed the spectacle for myself.

Arriving in the early evening, Simon opened up the tailgate and topper of his truck and stocked the game pocket of his hunting vest with water bottles. I turned on electric collars, their familiar ascending notes causing the dogs to yip and shake with excitement above and beyond their usual high energy for our runs. A metal dog box took up most of the truck bed. Simon beckoned Copa out of one of its carpeted compartments. Soon, she and another English setter, Charley, were collared up and on the ground. Simon said "Whoa!" as the setters held still at the field's edge, then pried apart two strands of a barbed wire fence and waved them through into the open field.

The setters accelerated away. Copa seemed to know precisely what she was supposed to do, and that it was her job to do it. She and Charley made big forays, heading off in different directions then circling and zig-zagging back across the land, combing the territory with diligence and seemingly in tandem. At times, the dogs disappeared into a patch of cover or a depression, then re-emerged, noses high, searching the air for the next scent. Our eyes tracked the white dogs as they rose up and down through the tall grass, focused and in flow. It was a beautiful sight, made more remarkable by how instinctual and intelligent it all seemed, the dogs sensing dimensions of this environment far beyond what Simon or I could perceive.

As we came to the fence line on the far side of the field, Copa appeared about to duck a wire onto the neighboring land. Simon pressed a button and Copa's collar let out a single beep, prompting her to turn and gaze toward him from a distance. Simon had explained that one beep means "check in" while two or more mean "come back here." With Copa checking in, Simon gave a hand signal, directing her to turn and stay on our friend's plot. She did. I'd been exposed to some of the language shared between Simon and Copa in our home. But this evening, I witnessed new and impressive examples of complex information being communicated between dog and trainer.

The land rose up beneath our feet. Once atop a subtle knoll, the wind picked up, bending the golden grasses and rattling sagebrush. Charley's sprint became a lope. Then he crept along, doubling back on a patch of cover. He turned into the wind and stopped, his tail suddenly rigid and nose hovering three inches above the ground. Copa sensed the action and came bounding toward us from another direction. "Whoa, Copa," Simon called out, yet young Copa already seemed to see Charley and process her role. She halted, freezing in place to the side and behind Charley, acting in support and synchronization.

I'd understood then that bird dogs pointed, but not yet how they backed one another, being willing to defer to the point of another dog out of devotion to the team. I admired the dogs' sophistication and sensibility of good-faith collaboration. It stood in contrast to many human dramas I knew, mine included, and underscored the wisdom of Simon's holding dogs in such high esteem.

Though it was before the season and we carried no guns, Simon gestured for the two of us to walk out in front of Charley's point. I followed with anticipation as Charley and Copa held their places with unwavering discipline. In a flurry, two Hungarian partridges took flight, peeling out to the side of us, their wings fluttering rapidly. Silhouetted in the low, amber light, they quickly angled down and away, cruising on to a patch of brushy cover. We walked the area further, but that seemed to be all that was there.

Copa and Charley drank water from bottles offered by Simon, who praised them as they panted and lingered for a moment. They looked self-satisfied. This is how upland hunting first came clear to me: through the magic of humans in relationship with dogs, us following them following their noses as they joyfully traced the land. I inhaled, grateful to be out in this open country together, glimpsing dynamics previously invisible to me. In the distance, shadows fell across the tan topography, accentuating its draws and folds which rose up to blue mountains, dwarfed under a broad and glowing sky.

Maeby

Proximity to the upland life came with new discoveries. While before, I only knew and loved Labrador retrievers, I came to appreciate the personalities of pointing dogs. Simon and I doted on them in sing-song voices, they cuddled up beside us when we got sick, and every now and then, while on a run, they bolted off until I tracked them down, usually miles away.

I learned how to cook game and shoot a shotgun. I came to relish clay shooting and its Annie Oakley marksmanship. I practiced mounting the gun, clicking off the safety, tracking the target with my eyes, pulling the trigger and following through all in one fluid motion. On his days off, Simon and I walked benches, draws, buttes, and mountainsides on remote grasslands, breathing in the landscape's timeless expansiveness.

I began carrying a gun as we walked. Simon trained me to hold my fire if I ever had doubt about the safety of dogs or people, insisting that I should never feel bad for passing up any shot. I listened, and held my fire so fastidiously that Simon's fellow guides affectionately dubbed me a "point and release hunter." One day afield, nearly all the birds flew my way and flushed high, holding up in the air far above the dogs, presenting safe and optimal shots. Still, I mounted my gun but did not shoot.

"What happened?" Simon finally inquired, smiling and curious.

"You said not to shoot if I have doubt," I said. "And I have doubt."

My doubt was complex, but no longer about safety, environmental protection, or even ethical treatment of animals. I'd explored and reasoned every angle. I knew I could trust my skills and awareness in the field. Simon's hunting lodge leased nearly a quarter million acres, rotating hunting grounds to steward target bird populations while protecting a wider web of life by keeping swaths of habitat from development. Reflecting on my "do no harm" childhood, wherein we'd gladly and unconsciously eaten inhumanely-raised grocery store meat, I'd come to see shooting a wild bird as far kinder and more courageous than paying to eat a bird raised and butchered on a conventional factory farm.

The only remaining question for me was whether to forgo meat altogether and become a vegan locavore, or take my place in the food chain in the mold of the

Greek goddess Artemis. In my logical brain, the ethical, reverent huntress route made sense, at least to try on for size. But in my heart, I still had doubt about the killing. Every time my finger touched the trigger, I found myself rooting for the birds, hesitant to consciously inflict suffering in a world already far too full of it.

I danced with this dissonance, always working to locate myself in the vortex of Simon's sporting pursuits. Our shared life and dogs were central to my heart and opened up new doors, yet I resisted sacrificing my selfhood on the altar of assimilation. Instead, I wanted to integrate it all into an authentic life path.

Questioning my balance one day, I sought the advice of a childhood friend, asking, "How do you know if someone is right for you?" His theory was that early on, things should be happy, easy, and uncomplicated, that couples should at least start with bliss, before the real responsibilities and challenges of life pile up.

"Huh," I said, recalling a recent incident where Simon and I had woken at four in the morning to a hunting dog splattering diarrhea across our bedroom carpet.

Among other developments in our outsized dog-owner life, when Copa turned four, Simon proposed breeding her. The idea was to have a DIY kitchen floor litter, keeping one puppy to raise and finding good homes for the others. One wrinkle was the timing of Copa's heat cycle and the wildly brief 63-day gestation period of dogs, as she'd likely deliver when Simon was away guiding. Though intimidated, I said yes, out of both nostalgia about the puppies of our youth and ignorance of all it would require. The caveat was that we would hire a vet tech friend to help midwife, and she quickly leaned in, painting baby animals on the wooden whelping box Simon built.

This time, rather than dogs flying in, semen was overnighted, that of a beloved male English setter who belonged to Simon's uncle. Copa thus artificially inseminated, we were told to expect a smaller-than-usual litter. Imaging suggested two pups in utero. Simon was away when Copa went into labor, wide-eyed, frenetic, and panting. Hours on, as Copa delivered two healthy puppies, my friend and I supported with sack-breaking, newborn puppy toweling-off, umbilical cord trimming and nursing support.

Once the action slowed, I followed the instructions of a dog delivery book and tried to coax Copa outside for fresh air. She stared at me, appearing impatient bordering on incredulous, not budging. Seconds later, she pushed out a third puppy, a shock so visceral to me and my midwife friend that we let out astonished screams of delight.

We kept the surprise runt, a white female with a black left ear. We named her Maeby, and from the start she gave us practice in navigating the unexpected. As a puppy, she played cat-and-mouse on runs to the point of annoyance. In disciplinary moments, after chewing a shoe or stealing food, she'd look at us side-eyed, as if unwilling to take our feedback too seriously. And yet, learning quickly from her veteran mother in the field, she turned on all the tenacity of her progenitors, while adding her own flare and independence to the mix. "Maeby she'll listen to you," we'd joke, "Maeby she won't."

The Women's Hunt

A year after Maeby was born, Simon and I got engaged. Feeling bittersweet, we made plans to move home to Vermont, Simon starting work at Orvis and me undertaking a graduate degree. As our time in Montana wound down, Simon expressed that though he was excited for the next chapter, he didn't think he'd ever feel ready to say goodbye to walking the prairie with the dogs each fall. Back in Vermont, we became the ones delivering our dogs out to Montana to hunt with guide friends and family who promised to keep them in touch with the land they loved.

One fall, when Copa was eight and Maeby four, I journeyed back to the waving prairie on my own, joining a women's hunt where Simon once guided. Our setters had left for Montana weeks before. As I arrived at the lodge around sunset, they greeted me with wiggles. I reciprocated with pets and forehead kisses, thrilled to be reunited. Still, it felt surreal and slightly lonely to return without Simon. Drinking in the pinks, purples and blues of faraway mountains, volcanic remnants that rose out of the grasslands like islands on a sea, I mused on whether I would have found myself in this beautiful place and pursuit if not for love of Simon and the dogs. Likely not, I decided.

The days were hot and it was hard going, made harder by my being seven months pregnant with our daughter. I brought a shotgun on the trip that Simon had given me, though I hadn't yet fully claimed it as mine. Although ostensibly for me, its purpose was also to be a loaner to friends joining Simon on hunts. I gladly shared it, relieved when others made proper use of it. Even if maximally ethical or keeping with fair chase principles, I still felt doubt about taking life. Yet, as I witnessed my power to grow life, I noticed a rising curiosity in me to explore the contours of my doubt.

One day of the women's hunt, I got to walk behind Copa and Maeby, my feet moving slowly but steadily over uneven ground and up steep hills, the spirit in my protruding belly lulled by the rhythm. On a rocky sidehill, Copa locked up on a point that Maeby backed. As I walked past their focused noses, three round, brown-and-white birds got up—native sharp-tail grouse. They sped away on my hunting partner's side, beyond where it was sporting or safe to shoot. I didn't mind, though. I felt so much kinship in witnessing our dogs at work.

On another afternoon as we walked atop a long, flat bench, I felt grateful to be covering gentler topography. Breathing in, I processed how we would likely pass down a hunting legacy to our children, how in carrying our child in utero here I already was. There arose in me a clarity that, despite the tensions of identity that might arise, I wanted to immerse myself in the full breadth of hunting, to fully know and consciously consider what we might impart.

On our way back toward the truck, the guide's English setter went on point 300 yards down a side slope. Catching up, I held my shotgun high and walked past the dog in sync with my hunting partner. The beat of sharp-tail grouse wings broke loose from the ground, a big covey flying up sporadically in ones, twos and threes. Zeroing in on a bird in range, I brought my shotgun up tight to my cheek, took off the safety and fired. The bird went limp and dropped through the air, indicating a clean kill, for which I was grateful. As more grouse got up, I broke open my gun, removing the spent shell and the unused one, content to watch the rest soar away.

As our guide gathered the bird from his retrieving dog who had rushed to find it upon being released, I felt I understood dogs anew. I saw the loyalty and love flowing between us as more clearly rooted in survival, harkening back to some remote tundra where our ancestors traded skills in food finding for a place by the fire and a share of the calories. This primordial sense did not detract, but deepened my sense of our bonds.

The guide, a seasoned naturalist, beckoned me closer. Using his hands to pull open the bird's throat, he extracted something from its crop. Opening up his palm, he held out a pile of undigested rosehips, red and round with feathery brown leaves. "Bird breakfast," he explained. I took the rosehips in hand, feeling their smoothness as I turned them over. Then I cupped my grouse, bill, my gaze landed on its delicate closed eyelids. It felt important to acknowledge the bird's sentience just moments prior, to thank it for the gift it gave in its death.

Returning to the truck, I followed the guide's instructions on how to field dress a bird, slicing across its lower abdomen and then pulling the bird's pungent yellowish entrails out of the still-warm cavity of its body. Later, despite the lodge's insistence that I didn't have to butcher my grouse, I went outside into the circling winds of the prairie with a knife, intent to fully step into the food chain and embody the role of apex predator.

I sliced my grouse along the breastbone on both sides. Tearing back the bird's skin, I carved deep maroon meat from its chest. The act felt gritty, but I began to see myself as a humble part of a greater ecology, with needs within it worthy of being met. All living things, myself included, came into view as less significant, yet more sacred. Careful to harvest all the meat I could, I set the sharp-tail breasts on a plate, my hands bloodied. Then I seared the meat on a grill, feeding myself and my unborn child from the land.

I didn't exactly overcome my doubt, but integrated it and began to see my self-reflection as a strength. *What if we all questioned the harm we cause and what we take to serve ourselves?* I wondered. It mattered to me to engage thoughtfully, mindful of the seriousness of my impacts. Although previously I had felt judgmental, even fearful, of the violence of upland hunting, I now pictured Simon in his former guide life up at the lodge processing birds. I understood the spirit behind it now, not as bloodthirst or glory, but reverence and duty.

I might still become a vegan, but I'm glad to have experienced what being a huntress entails, in all its self-sufficiency and complex interconnectedness. I found it deepened my comfort with death, and in so doing my comfort with life, too.

Phia

Our daughter Pippa was born that winter, and she took to upland life early and seamlessly. Once she could eat solid food, she gleefully and expressively ate game meat, much to Simon's family's delight. Among her earliest words were "Daddy boom birds."

Before Pippa turned one, Simon approached me about breeding Maeby. This time we both knew all the work a litter of puppies would require, especially with a baby to care for and work to juggle. I also now knew what pregnancy and birth and motherhood truly asks of mothers, and took seriously the potential impacts on our dog. Still, coming to understand the pattern that we would consider a litter of puppies once every five years or so, I liked the idea of keeping a torch lit through the generations.

The vet said Maeby had "definitely four, maybe five, possibly more" puppies in utero. True to form, she did the unexpected and delivered 10, prompting Simon to build an addition onto the whelping box. We helped the puppies nurse in two separate shifts so as to not overwhelm Maeby while making sure they all got what they needed to grow. When the puppies got bigger, a barely toddling Pippa cast a toy fly rod into their whelping box, giggling as the puppies chased a tuft of felt that she dangled on a line over their heads. We placed nine pups in doting homes. Again, we fell in love with the runt, a tiny female with a left eye patch and black dot on the top of her head where the hair spiked up into a subtle mohawk. We named her Phia, and, like Pippa, she was a natural.

The Family Hunt

Before long, we had a son named Willem. One fall when Pippa was three and Willem not yet one, our family returned to the Montana prairie, bringing all three generations of English setters along with us: Copa, Maeby and Phia. Following a dirt road, we drove up a draw to a high grassy plot overlooking the shimmering Missouri River, surrounded by fantastical-looking far-off buttes. Pulling over, we readied the family for a hunt. Simon stocked the game pocket of his vest with water bottles. Then he encouraged our English setters and retrieving dog, a black Lab, out of their dog box compartments and buckled GPS collars on them. I loaded Willem into a front pack on my chest where he could look outwards. Pippa climbed into a child carrier that I then hoisted on my back, all in all carrying 60 pounds of human cargo, plus water, snacks and layers.

Simon and I agreed he would hunt the perimeter of the plot while, for speed and safety considerations, I would walk a smaller circle inside and apart from him. Opening and closing a gate to cross a jackleg fence line, Simon followed the dogs through the golden field as I trudged along to the side and behind. Behind my head, Pippa called out the movements of the dogs like a sports announcer.

When one would temporarily dip out of sight, she'd cutely ask, "Where dey [they] go?" Willem kicked excitedly on my chest, vocalizing one of his first and favorite words, "dog," emphasis on the ending "guh" sound of the "g" ("daw-guh").

As Simon reached the far fence line, I grew tired. Having established a clear view of him as he began to circle back, the kids and I settled down on a rocky outcropping for a snack break, me quietly ensuring there were no prairie rattlesnakes about. After doling out snacks to now-contented children under the spackled shade of a bush, I began to see and mentally name native grasses like wheatgrass and fescue.

Taking in the prairie plants surrounding us, I noticed, as if for the first time, their intricate and ornamental leaves, blades, seedheads and blossoms, how the flora seemed to come in every imaginable color and texture. Catching fragrance in the air, I located silver sagebrush, admiring not just its smell but its silvery-green-blue tint and soft touch. I picked a sprig, letting our babbling son grasp it in his tiny fingers as he bounced on my knee. At once I was struck by how the prairie looks like an endless golden monoculture from afar, but how up close it is something different altogether—a diverse composition of life, its workings complex and enchanting.

Casting my eyes about in further botanical inventory, I observed orange leaves, then saw dangling from their slender dark brown stems a collection of round and gleaming red rosehips. Remembering the sharp-tail grouse I'd shot and the rosehips the guide had pulled from its crop, I reflected on how the rosehips fed the grouse, who fed me, who fed my child—how from the very start this land nourished my kin and made them strong. These connections clicked in my mind as beyond the physiological, extending to the emotional and spiritual as well. I gazed at our young daughter, who was breathing in the freedom of the open country, looking perfectly at ease.

Suddenly, I saw how the early alienation I felt with upland hunting had been transmuted into belonging. It began with the dogs pulling me across these wide open spaces. Here, I'd reckoned with my place in lineages of birds and the people and dogs who chase them. And now, as I breathed in the grassland botany, I felt awakened to the miraculous interplay of nature, coming into clearer view. Without upland hunting, I might not have been gifted this new way of seeing—considering the subtle yet powerful beauty of ecological exchanges, feeling connected to the land in ways I'd never anticipated. I felt tied to this place, myself a living part of its mystery. And I cherished it, grateful for a way back into the natural world we modern humans so often live estranged from.

Pippa was paying attention to her dad and the dogs. I was glad we could all witness Simon and the dogs in their element; but just as surely, I felt at peace at the deepening discovery of mine. Following her gaze, I saw Maeby off in the distance on point and young Phia coming into her own, patiently holding still behind. As Simon walked beyond them, a covey of grouse rose into a small, blue corner of the expansive sky.

Ulla

This past spring, Simon and I discussed another litter of puppies. While ever-devoted to our dogs, we were clear we'd hit a saturation point with our responsibilities piled atop years of pandemic seclusion, and considered that perhaps it was too much. Then, thinking aloud, Simon named how the kids were too young to remember the last litter. Now seven and four, he reasoned that if we waited until later, we might pass up on a window in their youth to share the magic of puppies—that which had so shaped us both from an early age in feeling kinship with and discovering the world. I returned to Simon minutes later, adamant, saying: "We have to do it."

Phia went into pre-labor around midnight. Simon and I slept on the couches by her whelping box, sleeping lightly and checking in frequently. Phia seemed to know precisely what to do and that it was her role to do it. By four in the morning, Simon and I were both awake, sleeves rolled up, helping deliver the first puppy. "Look," said Simon, "she has a black dot on her back just like Copa." Copa, the pup's 16-year-old great-grandmother with the identical back spot, was sleeping soundly on a dog bed nearby.

Six puppies were born in all. Halfway through the delivery, our kids woke up and came downstairs, taken aback by the mess but taking it all in. They showed concern as one smaller pup failed to rouse and cry at first, but then gained strength. I was glad they not only witnessed birth, but the fragility and resilience of life, and that their instincts were to care and root for its thriving as a value. As the puppies grew, four-year-old Willem, a spitting image of his mom at the same age, initiated games of chase with the puppies in the yard, running away in fits of giggles as they bounded after him.

Ultimately, we chose the first-born puppy and named her Ulla, placing the others in loving homes. We kept Ulla in large part because of her black back dot, an homage to Copa, the dog that started it all for us. We didn't set out to have a matriarchal line of four generations of English setters under one roof, but it's a special thing to see. I keep trying to line them up for a photo, but Ulla is too untrained and Copa too blind and deaf now to yet get all four to hold their places in tandem.

Though I spend many days in the field, I'm just as content to walk along without a shotgun. I'm still finding my authentic path through upland hunting pursuits, but I reflect on the distance I've traveled and how much love can prompt a person to evolve. For me, being open to growth brought me home to a truer version of myself.

We've been training Ulla, the kids asking her to "whoa" before she eats her kibble and cuddling with her on the couch, instructing her with a clear "no" when she mistakes them for chew toys. "Mom," said Pippa. "She's so soft and cute, it's like she has mind control over us." I laughed and agreed with her astute point, knowing well how affection for dogs can prompt people to go to remarkable lengths.

Epilogue

I've been taking the dogs out in the Vermont woods for runs lately, preparing them for bird season. Ulla's enthusiasm far outstrips her coordination, leading to clumsy and adorable misjudgments such as trips over logs as she races across the forest floor.

Copa's faculties, meanwhile, are fading. She loses track of us in the woods easily now, prompting us to frequently turn around and walk back to point her in the right direction. We find her, losing her way and looping circles, and finally get her attention with big waving arms or a loud and up-close call of "Here, Copa!" Still, she bounds up and down through fields, nose engaged, with an elderly version of the same spring in her step that she's always had. I pass her sleeping around the house and have to check for the subtle rise and fall of her ribcage to confirm that she's still with us.

It's autumn as I write this. Soon, Simon will leave on a road trip back to central

Montana to walk its open country with the dogs. We all suspect Copa's holding on until then, her heart's last desire to be with him chasing birds. This time, when Simon leaves with her for the prairie, I'll be glad to see them go.

Accidentally bewitched as I was by this upland life, I know what it can do for the soul.

Michael L. Neiduski
On Love and Bird Dogs

I didn't get into bird dogs to fall in love, but I did anyway.

I didn't get into bird dogs to have my heart ripped out of my chest either, but here I am, scarred and stitched and stapled, blood still pumping, compelling me to chase points and birds, to seek the enchanting places and people where they all come together.

I'm going to let you in on a little secret—no one gets out unscathed. But, I'm getting ahead of myself.

It started on fawn legs, as all first dates do—wobbly, unsure, wide-eyed, and skeptical. How do you know you picked the right one? It's not very helpful when they don't talk back much. But, you pick. You hug, and if you're that type of person, you kiss and you let the nuzzle and the warmth and the potential override the fear and trepidation, and you take them home.

You commit to building a life, a routine. Sometimes you sleep together right away, others hold space and build trust. Let me assure you, there's no right answer here, regardless of what all the books and podcasts and talking heads will tell you. No matter what, at some point, there's coalescence. A coming together. A moment that says, "Let's do this," and you mean it. Both of you.

It was a cold, wet, shivery drive home when we had that moment. It poured all day while we chased birds, but we were young and dumb and didn't give a damn. We were soaked to the bones with the heat on high and the defroster struggling to keep up with the humidity rising off our bodies and clinging to the windows of the truck cab. She fell asleep on my chest the moment we got home and dried out, softly heaving sounds asleep. Content.

We had our moments, our tiffs. Communication wasn't always clear—it sometimes came out jumbled. Sometimes, she just went her own way, even when she knew damn well what I asked of her. It was a good reminder to let her have her head, to loosen the reins a bit and trust what was unfolding. It's necessary to admit you don't always know best. It's also hard.

We mustered our courage and took trips to places we'd never been: Northern Wisconsin, Minnesota, Kansas, Texas, Oklahoma and Vermont. Some of those were one-offs, others became tradition. Some trips we took in groups, some with one other couple, and sometimes it was just the two of us. Long drives down pencil-straight highways during which she'd sleep most of the time but always touching me, that longing for connection ever present. It was like that until the end. But, we're not there yet.

We made friends all over, as two who are as close as us are prone to do. Invites here, day dates there. Come stay a while. It'll be a good time. Even for others, it was hard to resist that big smile and the way she leaned into your attention. She knew exactly how to make you feel like you were the only thing around.

But if she didn't like you, Lord, look out. Fire and brimstone and gnashing teeth were at the table and you were on the menu. One morning, she lay sleeping on the floor at the cabin up north. We were lazy, and the coffee was hot while the wind blew cold outside. Our friend Taylor learned of her temper the hard way. While she slept, he crept under the full-head, teeth-baring bear rug and slid his way close to her. Before I could warn him, he inhaled and let out his best roar.

She sprung away in a panic, but it only took milliseconds to get her bearings. To this day Taylor thanks me for the wherewithal I had to grab her in the moment of recognition and hold on tight. She gave me her best, "Let me at him!" attempts, and finally gave in. Thankfully, she had a large heart and forgave as quickly as she raged.

I'd like to say we lived happily ever after, that the long rides and the sunsets and the wild places went on forever. Who wouldn't want an endless stream of talks on the tailgate and splitting fries from the drive-thru on the way home. I know I did.

She died in my arms this past spring, but not the way you think. Not the way an old dog goes when they've clung on as long as they can and are just grateful you're there to hold them one more time. She didn't get that luxury, and if I'm honest, I'll never forgive myself for that.

She died in my arms as I sprinted to the nearby creek in desperate hope of cooling her off. But it was too late. The sun and the sudden heat of the day had their hold of her and there was nothing I could do to free her from the jaws of death.

I wish it was a joke like that bear rug prank, but it's not.

I got divorced pretty soon after that, too.

See. No one gets out unscathed.

I've after-actioned every angle of that afternoon and the aftermath that came with it, and this is what I've settled on. No one gets out unscathed.

Do this long enough, do this in a way where you give a shit, where you take the leaps of faith, where you take the trip and put yourself out there, and there is going to be some hurt along the way.

OK, not some. A whole fucking lot.

It's part of the deal. That moment you pull the pup out of the whelping pen and claim it as your own, you write the check with a part of you knowing you could get your heart broken. Ignore it all you want, but it's there.

How do you come back from it when the receipt finally comes due?

I remember, the grouse season after I left Wisconsin was my worst ever. From a numbers perspective it was awful, but I'm not talking about days hunted (way less) or birds flushed, even though that was the down year that broke the cycle, and no one quite knew what happened. Moreso, it was my worst in the mouthful-of-feathers sense. I couldn't get her one and I hated it.

She had just come into her own, and I became the bad partner. For all those times I told Roy or Taylor or Jerry that I didn't think she would cut it, that I didn't think she'd make it as a grouse dog, here she was running and pointing her ass off in the woods; I used to call home. I didn't kill but a woodcock or two over the course of that trip. Gone were the months of weekends we spent in those woods all we had that year was three days and I couldn't get it done. But she didn't care.

"Keep going, there's more. I've got your back," was her mantra, her daily affirmation.

"What are you twiddling your thumbs for? Let's go."

That spirit, that affirmation, served us well, even if it got us in trouble now and again, including that first trip north after moving south. Those last-day, last-walk, I'm-not-ready-to-be-done-yet decisions tend to be hero or zero like that.

To round out the trip we decided to hit "The End of the Road," a cut so originally named for a dirt that abruptly ended at the start of a spruce bog with an aspen cut running down one side and back along the path we drove in. We always started at the bog and this day was no different.

We made the walk and it wasn't fruitless—one more woodcock in the bag. I have a video of her happily bringing it back to me in her signature loping gait. She always had a timely return, but trust me, she also rushed for no one. A "here you go, I've got your back" grin across her muzzle.

We were down to the wire. Cut bait and head for the truck, the cooler and the gun case and calling it over, or take the wide loop right down the far ridge, cut through the valley and hunt the other side along the road back to the end.

Keep going, there's more.

Except there wasn't. Not the more we wanted anyway.

I suppose this is where I should interject that she came from strong German roots. That may explain her willingness to square off with a man in bear's clothing. In a world where you can choose to fight or be nice, when it came to furry things, even if they are covered in thousands of pointy quills, she chose to fight. Every time.

It took a while for Taylor and me to hold her still and get everything out we could reach. The roof of her mouth, her tongue, gums, all over. We let her up after thorough inspection and there she stood, wondering why we hadn't started walking yet as we put multi-tools away and kicked ourselves for making one last push. She didn't care. She hunted all the way to the truck like nothing happened at all, her tail swishing back and forth to the same beat of Dory singing, "Just keep swimming, just keep swimming."

I still smile thinking about it. I smile in that wry way one does when they're being taught a lesson they're not quite ready to accept.

Sometimes, that's the only way to process it. To smile and think of the lessons learned and move forward. I don't think about her death much anymore, but I spend a lot of time mulling over those lessons. Oftentimes they pop up when I least expect them to.

She was known by many for her retrieves. If you hit a long bomb, you wanted her on the ground. She had a way of summoning cripples to hand from the ether. My buddy Ed still tells the story about the waffled rooster we tag-teamed that coasted out over a bean field and disappeared. I took off after it with her in tow; in short order, here she came with it. I swear she winked at me when I took the bird—"I've got your back."

She didn't point her last wild rooster, and she didn't care. Taylor dumped it on a long crosser in a giant patch of wild sunflower. When he shot, a covey of bobs erupted at our feet, and he lost our bearings. I was convinced that rooster was gone to the coyotes.

You'd think after all that time we spent together I'd have faith in her to bring it back, but I still doubted. True to form, her last wild mouthful of feathers was another act of proving me wrong.

One last act to say, "I've got your back."

I've done my fair share of doubting since last spring. Since she left. For a while I doubted whether I deserved another dog. I doubted if I even wanted to hunt much this season. I didn't think I'd enjoy it.

It's been a lot of rebuilding, in dogs and in life. Loss will do that to you, make you question, make you wonder. It piles on the doubt in the quiet moments until it's almost too much to carry. But the heart is like any other muscle, when torn and forced to rebuild, it comes back stronger, more resilient.

I went back to Kansas this season. I went back to the spot of that last retrieve and went for a walk. The quail were still there, but the roosters were gone. There I stood, wind ripping across grass and wheat stubble and that giant patch of native sunflower and I watched her watch the young dog out front drinking the wind while her hair feathered out around her face like the tail of a good setter hard on point. She looked back at me and smiled in wonder.

I thought about Plexi, my wirehair now gone. I thought about the stitches on my heart and the quills and the retrieves and all the things she taught me in between.

Keep going. There's more. I've got your back.

Reid Bryant
Autumn's Eve

In September, the summer people left. They hauled their boats and turned them bottoms up to the weather. They put the better ones in sheds. They tied Clorox bottles to their mooring lines and left plenty of scope for the ripping ice of winter. They pulled water intakes from the lake and drained the pipes, shuttered the windows and padlocked the doors. They left keys hidden under rocks only they would remember.

Kelly loved to see them go. She loved when the lake became hers again. The loons and the barred owls, mere spectacles to the summer folk, became in September eccentric relatives singing drunkenly into the night. She cherished the evenings when the first wood fire cut the chill in the lake house, when she could fold the wool blankets at the foot of her bed, rejoicing in their scratchy weight, that mothball-and-sheep smell. And finally, amidst all the tokens of summer's end, Kelly gave up her daily swim.

That year she gave it up well within sight of Columbus Day. She missed the catch-your-breath cold of the morning, and the way her skin pimpled when she pulled herself onto the lakeside ramp of rock to towel off. Her skin went tight as she rubbed the blood back into it, and she'd look at her body and remember how it had been when she was young. Standing there wrapped in a towel, she'd close her eyes and revisit a body unfamiliar with things like wrinkles and creaking knees and fingers gone crooked from use.

That fall, with the swim a thing of the past, the early mornings bore an unscripted freedom, and there was room for a second cup of tea. Kelly carried her mug to the sleeping porch, where she sat in the quiet and yodeled at the loons. A single warble rang back from the cove in the east, and Kelly smiled. She'd always been able to conjure a response. There'd been a pair on the lake in summer for as long as she could recall, even in the years when everything else seemed lean.

Kelly never worried after the loons' return, just as she never put much stock in the lean times. There always seemed to be just enough of everything:

partridge and deer in the woods, togue in the deep troughs of the lake, a suitor or two who'd come around to vie for her hand. Those silly men and their grand gestures…picking up the electric bill or offering to re-roof the place, as if such things might win her. She took what they gave, and thanked them in her way, and encouraged them off down the road when she deemed their debts were squared. Then it was just Kelly again, and the call of the loons in the morning. And in fall, as if exposed by the silence of departed summer folk and barren trees, there was True Rattray.

Teasing True Rattray was one of the few things Kelly'd loved steadily and vigorously her whole life. But tease wasn't quite the term for the pokings and proddings that Kelly gleefully doled out on her lifelong friend. What Kelly loved to do was tempt True Rattray, and rattle him off that narrow way upon which he'd long chosen to walk. Sometimes, in the quieter moments, she even wondered if she hadn't sculpted her own life as a taunting antithesis to True's own.

True was a good man, born of a line of apple growers who recorded their genealogy in the gnarled old limbs of the family orchard; who worked the year through in their clean white shirts and flat-soled boots. True lived where he grew up: on the sprawling place just east of Kelly's, picking and pruning and pressing, tending the trees planted by his great-grandfather, Wallingford. Nearly 400 acres of rich, black loam tumbled down to the edge of Swan Lake, as well-tended a Maine farmstead as ever there was. Generations of Rattray men had proudly kept it so, bending to their work through the changing times alongside the hard-handed women who loved them obliquely until they went to rest in the cemetery on the hill.

True had the broad shoulders of his father, though his back was bent from the weight of a lifetime of autumn-heavy harvest bags. He worked six days and went to church on the seventh, and he kept his trees pruned—they were as graceful as dancers. And his tools were well-oiled and sharp. He grew the finest apples in that apple-growing region, and his fruit was known throughout Maine, as were the cider and donuts he sold at the fair each October. He was a good and simple man. The tourists, insensitive to the beauty of good and simple things, considered True only occasionally, if ever, as little more than a pinch of Maine salt.

Kelly had learned long ago that there was nothing quite so wonderful as tempting True Rattray. There was something irresistible in wielding a devilish power over him, watching him come up against the attitude that trapped him so neatly between well-laid lines. When just a girl, she stood summer Sundays at the split-rail fence dividing their properties, calling out to the boy she knew was kneeling to quiet prayer inside. "True Raaaaaaaaatraay," she'd call in that singsong voice. "Come on out here and let's go fishing...I got a can of worms all duuuuh-uuuhg."

In later years she'd upped the ante, standing naked and dripping on that ramp of rock where she'd announce her morning swim. "Hey, True. Come for a swim. The water's as cool and clear as the River Gihon." She stood there all the longer when she knew True was picking the lower orchard, hidden in the trees that looked out over the lake to the south and west. She stood there and felt his eyes on her, felt the weight of conscience that hung like an apple bag from his shoulders, and she smiled and called. The loons might call in response, or the first breath of day might rustle the leaves, but she never got an answer from True Rattray.

True Rattray had a single weakness, one that Kelly shared: partridge. True and Kelly had grown up together amid the splendor of a land regaining itself. With every passing year, more and more of the hillside farms around the lake were abandoned, divided, sold or simply left fallow, as the farmers tried and failed to convince sons and daughters not to leave. But in the desertion of the potato fields and orchards and mowings, a wealth of partridge emerged. In the popple whips and grown-over orchards, True and Kelly watched generation upon generation of partridge swell to bursting, and through their youth they'd harvested their share.

But in the glow of those autumn woods they'd also grown to love the land and the birds and each other. It was a love so elemental and clean that it held no passion, just a thrumming resonance. And it grew as they did and stuck them close, pinned to each other and to the stubble-grown hillsides and the whirr of brown birds fast departing. And aware as they were of it all through the years, they were never tempted to overstep their respective roles.

That morning near Columbus Day, Kelly left the sleeping porch, and put her empty mug in the sink. She saw her reflection in the kitchen window, and the splash of color that hovered behind it, or through it, and she saw that she was old. Her brown hair was sandy and finer than it had been, but her eyes were still black and sparkling. She returned a crinkly smile to her reflection, and said out loud, "Well, if this old bag of bones can't tempt True with the sins of the flesh, then I suppose I'll have to make do with stronger stuff."

She walked to the gun case and opened it, and took out the little Dickson double. It was a beautiful gun, a gift well out of proportion from the one man she'd dared to marry. In some ways, perhaps, it was fair dowry for the years she'd traded to society life, to the house in Boston and the formal dresses and the cocktail parties on the Hill. He'd bought her the gun so they could hunt the Maine woods together on weekends, and they'd done so happily for a few years. But when business began to tether him, and the firm grew richer and more complex, autumn weekends became Kelly's alone. She didn't mind. She liked the quiet and the space in the big bed, and she loved the little gun. Pretty soon she simply stopped returning home when the weekends ended, and the marriage dissolved as gently as sand through dust-dry fingers.

She cracked the gun and checked the bores, pocketed a fistful of shells, tucked the gun under her arm, and walked to the door, where she took her Woolrich shirt from its peg and mashed a tattered red crusher onto her head. Outside, the morning was silvery with overcast, and slick with moist leaves on the dirt road. Kelly turned, walked back to the kitchen, and from the bowl on the table grabbed an apple, a Cox's Golden Pippin. Each fall she stole them from the ancient tree overhanging the Rattray's fence. She polished the apple against the coarse wool of her shirt, slipped it in her pocket, and smiled as she closed the door.

Kelly no longer stopped at True's gate. She'd given up any formality with him before she'd ever attempted any, and she knew it irked him. She swung into his dooryard and began warbling her singsong. "True Raaaaaaaaatraay, come on out. No use wasting as fine a day as this…" No answer. She walked on down to the lower orchard, where she saw two flat-soled boots poking from the crown of an apple tree. She walked over and grabbed the ladder, and leaned on it enough to make it jiggle.

"By Golly, Kelly, haven't you learned yet to stop torturing me? If you send me crashing to the ground it's you who'll be fixing my meals and mending my wounds and doing all my work. And you and I both know you have a longstanding allergy to work."

He descended the ladder and set the full apple bag on the ground and straightened up, stretching his back. He looked Kelly full in the face. He couldn't help but smile at her devilry.

"So what exactly are you after with that thunderstick? Hoping to get yourself a bear before they go to ground?"

"True Rattray, I came to ask you to go on a partridge walk with me." Kelly's eyes twinkled. "You know how I'm getting on, and my arthritis is acting up, and I can just tell that a pot of partridge soup will set me straight. Besides, we both know that half the young birds in Maine are stacked up in those abandoned trees on your hillside, and that you'd like nothing more than to join me in shooting them.

"All work and no play makes True a dull boy, and besides," she said, feigning concern, "it could be dangerous for a little old lady up there…"

True took off his hat and scratched his head. He turned and looked over his shoulder at the west hillside, where a section of old orchard had been abandoned in his youth. There were birds aplenty up there, he knew, and in the early season the young coveys would still be intact. It would make for some easy shooting.

"Jeezums, Kelly. Bird hunting on a Thursday morning. Look at these trees! I got bushels more to pick and a truck coming tomorrow for a load. I can't see how to find the time."

He looked at the ground, kicked a half-rotten drop, and looked back at the hillside again. "I been seeing some birds, though."

Kelly knew she had him.

"If you're saying you'd send a gimpy old lady out into the woods alone, you're certainly not the gentleman I thought I knew, True Rattray. Let's hope this is where you want to be when the good Lord returns. And while you're doing all that work you seem so set upon, I'll gladly cut your partridge population down to size."

And with that she turned and marched a few steps, leaving True toeing the grass at his feet. Kelly looked back.

"True, while I'm gone, enjoy this." She pulled the apple from her pocket and chucked it to him underhand. He caught it awkwardly.

"Cox's Golden Pippin." He said it matter-of-factly. "Only one fellow hereabouts grows these."

"True Rattray, the spirit is willing, but the flesh is weak." Kelly giggled and walked out the gate, dropping two shells into her gun.

The morning turned drizzly. Up there on the hillside, Kelly stood on the carpet of slick fallen leaves, a kaleidoscope of color that seemed to radiate light. She looked off over the lake, and could see a corner of her little house and where the side road met the tar. She could see True's orchard, and the crisp lines of his house, and his fence, and the stone walls he kept mended and straight. It was all so beautiful, and as full of everything she needed as it was empty of people.

Save one. True Rattray's white shirt stood out against the swath of muted greens in the orchard. She couldn't see the details, but she knew he was at work.

A loon called out from the lake, and Kelly answered, and the loon answered back. She turned back to the brushy edge of the abandoned hillside. Walking in among the old trees, moving slowly, she'd not gone ten feet when she heard that *chirp-chirp chirrr-chirp* right up ahead, and then thunder roaring, and a flash of movement.

It was just movement, though, a blur of brown briefly visible, leaving in its place only leaves gently falling. She never even mounted the gun. Instead, she aimed the little Dickson towards the ground and fired both barrels. She ejected the spent hulls and pocketed them, giggled again, and said out loud, "That'll get you thinking, now won't it, True Rattray?"

She reloaded, then struck off again in joy, ever deeper into the autumn hillside.

Marissa Jensen
Steady Yeti
The Beauty of Second Chances

A strike to the face, teeth pulling hair, nails scraping at my clothes and skin. She came at me from all directions. The innocent, tender face from the other side of the glass door turned into a demogorgon the moment she came inside. It was clear at that moment, this six-month-old German shorthaired pointer had never been told no. But as I stood there, mopping up the assortment of superficial scratches and bites, I thought to myself, "This little dog is going to leave a permanent imprint on my heart. It's the tough ones who always do."

Sucker. Pushover. A softie, and easily persuadable. I can't—or refuse—to say no to an animal in need. For years, I've watched pets relinquished due to cost or illness, or behaviors seemingly beyond repair. The life of an ER veterinary technician tried to mold me into something jaded and scarred. But my story is a testimony to the beauty of second chances. Adopted at birth, I never knew life before my family, but I am grateful and thankful each day for the woman who knew she couldn't and for the family that prayed day in and day out that they could.

Regardless of my past and the litany of excuses I drum up, all it took was a few pleading calls from a pup's former owner for me to cave and agree to take her home.

To my credit, I said no, multiple times. The first call that came through was a request to purchase the puppy. The owner didn't have time and she wasn't a good fit for the family, but she came from excellent bloodlines. With two other German-bred dogs at home, one pointed-eared and the other floppy, my hands were more than full, and I wasn't in need of another bird dog.

Another call and another emphatic no, but anyone listening nearby likely detected the beginning of a tremor in my tone. Eventually, his calls took on a different timbre and the pup's owner was at his wit's end. She needed to go, would I be willing to come and get her as soon as possible?

Ultimatums and frustrations were palpable from his end of the line and the next thing I knew, I was jamming my keys into the ignition and cursing under my breath as I headed their way.

After the initial shock at her behavior, I begrudgingly loaded up the thirty-pound bundle of fire and fur and thanked her previous owner for trusting me with her care. Slamming my hatchback closed, I began to entertain a sense of possibility for her future and what it could mean for my own.

On the drive home, I loudly and profusely promised myself and my son that I would remain resolute in my intention of rehoming her. This was only temporary. But of course, the only person I was lying to was myself.

There were problems that needed to be addressed immediately, so she had to stay, for now. A fierce urinary tract infection explained the housebreaking concerns. The anxious energy that sparked her jumping, biting, and screaming for attention would need to be redirected in a somewhat healthier manner. She was desperate for attention; she just didn't know how to ask for it. Regardless of all these concerns, I saw something special in her eyes. This beautiful monster had a strong desire to please, and I was excited to give her the opportunity.

A good friend and a mentor from my humble bird hunting beginnings had initially encouraged me to take on this pup. He knew her lines well and promised she would be worth the time and effort. So once again, we loaded up and made our way down a dusty, gravel road toward Phillips Gun Dogs, to channel her raw energy into birds.

I'll never forget the first time I watched her work. Head down, front feet planted, and tail pointed to the sky. Her blood ran thick with the history of bird dogs past, and I sat back and admired the beauty of quality breeding as she nailed a planted quail. My resolve to rehome her started to waiver, but still, I stubbornly refused to call her mine. Regardless, watching her hold this bird steady is a bird hunter's dream. I ticked off seconds in my head as I watched my friend kick around the brush in front of him. Her intensity never faltered, and her focus never wavered. Finally, more to my relief than the others, the bird flushed, and this steady little pup held her ground.

That night when we returned home, she decided to make her claim. She snuck in bed and curled up beside me, those soft eyes finding mine. With a head pat and a smile, it was decided. Yeti was officially home.

None of the dogs who call my house a home came to me without a previous owner. And with each past, they bring new stories, uniquely and beautifully their own. Some of our dogs' beginnings were tough, and some simply landed with us due to life and unfortunate circumstances. Some have found new homes where they can shine, while a select few called our house home the moment they arrived. Our home has become a sanctuary built upon second chances with each life a new chapter and a story that isn't finished being written.

Over the next year, as I worked with Yeti, I found something beautiful behind her anxiousness and high energy. Yeti was sensitive and soft toward her handler. She would do anything to please if just given the opportunity. For a long time, I worried this softness would be a struggle and that a simple and unintentional overcorrection would fail her. However, our time together revealed an immense strength that lay within that softness. She was willing to give me whatever I asked of her, and it was up to me to be responsible for this. To own a soft dog is to recognize the importance of providing guidance, without asking for too much.

This revelation sparked another—when I look at this little dog, I see a reflection of myself. We each hold a strong desire to please, but sometimes at a detriment to ourselves. It's a reminder that giving all of yourself to others leaves you with an empty tank. Perhaps it's merely a projection, anthropomorphism at its best, but there's a lot about this little dog that reminds me of myself, and we've bonded in ways that were unexpected and refreshing.

Yeti became a rock in my life, and upon the unexpected loss of our family's beloved German shepherd, I clung desperately to this little roan-colored dog. It was at this moment that she allowed me to truly hold onto her, as she lay calmly and quietly by my side. Grief is our mind's way of searching for love, and I found solace as she lay there beside me.

A full season would pass before I felt confident enough to run Yeti with our older and more seasoned bird dog. Previously, self-doubt drove me to the uplands with only one kennel loaded up, leaving another dog frustrated and angry at home. With time, I found the confidence to handle both dogs, and now I can't imagine experiencing the uplands in any other way.

Our first group hunt together is one I'll never forget. Just the dogs, moving in harmonized grassland beauty to the beat of our own drum. The covey of bobwhites I cut my teeth on became Yeti's introduction to wild quail. A staunch point and an honor from Reese, her partner, gave me the opportunity to pull up on the future of our collective hopes and dreams.

That first morning together, I learned the intricacies of each of my dog's styles. Reese ranged further out with wide, sweeping casts. Yeti worked closer, meticulously, picking up each individual scent. As the day grew longer, so did her distance. As she ranged out, the more our confidence grew in one another. I stopped looking down at my GPS unit and let my trust in her soar.

However, as with everything in life, our time together hasn't been perfect. It's easy to paint a story through rose-colored glasses, but that's unrealistic and quite frankly, a lie.

Outside of the field is where Yeti's anxiety is most prevalent. It can make her too much for some to handle, and there are many days this undirected energy and nervousness puts my teeth on edge. But we continue to grow together, both in the field and at home. We've traveled to uplands inside and out of state lines. She's tested my patience, as I'm sure I've tested hers, but we continue to learn and move forward in a synchronized steadiness that's paralleled to none.

I screw up more often than not, but Yeti forgives me, and I try harder to make up for my mistakes. She should have multiple species under her belt by now. I suppose technically she does, but my subpar shooting and lack of confidence have led to missed opportunities and holes in what I thought would make up a catalog of "perfect memories."

But memories aren't bag limits or a bird in hand. Memories are tangible moments of beauty that you can taste and touch and hear when you look back over the years. I remember the sight of just her tail, deep in a ravine on her first pheasant. I can feel the heat from the afternoon sun as she brings me her bird with a mouthful of feathers.

I feel a ghost-tingling sensation of cold in my fingers, and I hear the crunch of snow breaking beneath the weight of our journey when I reflect on a late-season walk for quail.

It's because of my dogs that I love the uplands, and it's because of the uplands that I own my dogs. One cannot exist without the other, and I can't imagine my life without either. I'm no beginner to working dogs, with years of handling canines searching for a scent and a purpose other than birds. Still, I consider myself a novice handler, and likely always will. The moment we believe ourselves an expert is the moment we let our dogs down.

We've since added feathers and firsts to our vests with each season, and I watch with pride as her devotion and purpose grow toward our 13-year-old boy. Together, they've made new memories in the field as I looked on smiling, knowing their success makes me happier than any I could've made on my own. It's these constants—the love of family and a good bird dog—that remind us of what's important. The steadiness that comes with time and age helps us keep life's ever-growing list of priorities straight. And it's because of a certain soft, unwanted bird dog, one I almost passed up, that I remember an important message about life.

There is a beauty that lies in second chances. With love and kindness, all things can thrive.

Eric Thompson
The Best is Still to Come

What compels my outdoor journey is the promise of the unexpected, the unanticipated the moments that catch me off balance, and make me consider what I hadn't before.

My journey has been a long one. It started in a little yellow house set back off the main road and hidden by a cluster of trees. The house was located west of the four-way on McCully Mountain, near the small town of Lyons, Oregon, which in turn sits on the west slope of the Cascades.

Our house overlooked Jordan Valley, a landscape quilted in shades of green and the occasional square of brown. All around were the telltale signs of agriculture and logging, activities that created thriving habitat for some wild things, of which I was one. The landscape fostered a childhood spent running unencumbered through the woods, across the fields, and along the creek bottoms. It fostered a wanderlust that finds me always looking over the next ridge.

The Willamette Valley played a pivotal role in the history of bird hunting in North America. It was one of the first regions where introduced pheasants would eventually take hold and produce a wild population. The valley became a popular hunting destination, and it maintained a healthy population of birds for most of the 20th century.

By the time I was old enough to hunt alone, however, those storied days were coming to an end. The birds were scarce and well-educated; those residual pockets of wild pheasants and quail had to be sniffed out along the bramble-choked ditch lines, unsprayed fence rows, and tangled creek bottoms. I made it my mission to find them. I recruited my high school buddies in this effort, and as a group, we devoted the hours after school and every weekend of the season to combing miles of farmland in search of wild birds. We were a rag-tag bunch, and we followed behind whatever dog was willing and available to bust the brush ahead of us.

On a cold November morning in 1989, I headed out with a few members of this crew. The day was slow to start, and we were only able to produce a few quail as we worked a fence line that was losing a long battle with the encroaching blackberry vines, grasses and hardwood saplings. Nearing the slough that bordered the back of the property, my buddy's Vizsla locked up on a patch of wild rose. We spread out to cover the escape routes, and Brandon went in for the flush.

I'd been ready for more quail, but what rose before me was this gaudy antithesis, cursing and climbing and completely unexpected. I could hear the wingtips scraping brush, and a wily old rooster exploded out of the thicket, chucking like his tail was on fire. The bird broke cover beating hell for leather, and we stood there half stunned at this unexpected sight. The rooster emerged from the left side of the bramble and let its quickening wingbeats move it across the front, using the roses for cover. I snapped out of my stupor as it rounded the corner in front of me. My gun slid up to my shoulder as my eyes tracked the bird's path, and right before his wings locked up for the glide, I pulled the trigger.

Years and distance temper the excitement I felt that day, and I look back now on a memory of me bagging my last ever wild Willamette Valley pheasant. The end of an era passed in a plume of falling feathers, the receding thrill of the chase, and youth's incapacity to consider what might come next, or what might never be again. Fortunately, the birds of my home range fueled a fire that compelled me, as I grew older, to look for birds in as many places as I could. As the mid-80s saw a significant period of decline in pheasant populations across Oregon, chukar partridge, another introduced Eurasian species, had a population explosion across the state's central and eastern high desert. My first opportunity to hunt chukar came on a pheasant and quail hunt in Central Oregon. My brother-in-law, Tony, suggested we go a couple of miles up the Deschutes River drainage to hunt chukar. That afternoon we packed up Doc, his aging Lab/Weimer mix and headed to the rimrock.

The day was remarkable, and the sheer numbers of birds we put up that afternoon made for limits all around and one tired, old dog. As first chukar hunts go, that hunt was hard to beat, and one against which I'd measure all other hunts. At thirteen or fourteen, I imagined every chukar hunt would be the same; in hindsight, I was still too green to yet understand that there will always be those glory days that require time and distance to achieve perspective. Had I known how significant chukar hunting would become to me, I may have urged my brother-in-law and other family members to spend a few more days in that hard country in that season when the birds were abundant.

Chukar hunting is why I wander the West. In the name of chukars, I have put thousands of miles on my truck, my boots and my dogs. Chukars have lured me to the far-flung corners of Oregon, to places off the beaten path, to regions most people would never explore. In pursuit of chukars I have found petroglyphs, seams of gemstones in the bedrock, and hidden water sources. I've been drawn into easily-overlooked places that are too far, or too steep—places where even those few who do go looking rarely find what they are after. I've come to rely on the unexpected.

Chukar hunting can be a solitary pursuit. Even when hunting with friends, we can find ourselves hundreds of yards, if not miles apart. The solitude leaves time to soak up the surroundings, to become familiar with that choreography of birds and dogs. In chukar country, things get simple: there is no pressure outside of the need to breathe, and to continue to follow the dogs. You can lose yourself in the long moments of quiet. That is, until a dog goes on point.

A chukar flush can be composed of much more than the rush of birds taking wing. When the dog goes on point, a chukar hunter must move without delay. Chukar are notoriously uncooperative. Given the opportunity, they will run, then stop in the most difficult-to-reach places. They prefer locations that require hunters to work way uphill, over hundreds of yards of rugged terrain and sometimes even snow. During these climbs, the heart pounds hard and fast, not so much out of excitement but as in effort to pump oxygen to the far-flung reaches of the body.

When I hunt chukars, my lungs protest and my legs burn as I move uphill, across shifting rocks and over uneven slopes. At length, if I am lucky, I'll be greeted by the sight of my dog, Hex, on point, a few yards off the edge of a scree slide or rimrock. She possesses that stiff-tailed, eyes-on-the-prize, not-even-winded point. She lets me know she's done her job and now it's time to do mine.

On a cold, clear November day in Eastern Oregon, my GPS alerted me that Hex was on point three-hundred-thirty-six yards uphill. I adjusted my line and moved toward her location. Making my way, I tried not to fall or twist a knee, and I crested a ridge to find her. Seeing her on point changed everything: the gulping breaths from the ascent were replaced with calm, even, oxygen-rich breaths; the burning legs reverted to a sure, steady gait that anticipated the flush. I picked a line below Hex, following a game trail. Each step was solidly placed, a foundation from which I could steady myself in the split second those birds would give me to get my gun into position to fire.

Right on cue, three birds exploded like rockets from the middle of the slide, wings blurry as they raced downhill, adding speed with each second, plunging towards the safety of the next ridge and canyon below. My gun came up, and I fired. The sounds of the chukars' wingbeats as they took to the air, and the sound of my shotgun firing, became complementary even though they existed on two separate planes. In my mind, minutes passed between the birds taking flight and one tumbling amongst the rocks as its covey mates glided to safety far below. But, before I could lower the gun, six more birds rose in unison from 30 yards up the slide to present a quick left-to-right passing shot. Again, the gun sounded, and a bird fell. This was a cinema of hours playing out in seconds and heartbeats, reinforcing the sentiment that resounds with any hunter of birds that covey: never expect that every bird has flushed until every bird has.

Through the excitement of birds flushing, guns firing and birds falling, Hex maintained her inventory of all birds downed. She was still on point, but her muscles quivered with anticipation of the release to complete her job. A command of "Hunt dead!" freed her from the trance and she made her way to the first bird marked. It took little effort to find, but the changes in her body language were wonderful.

I have described how I feel watching Hex hunting in earnest, but that feeling doesn't compare to what I experience when I watch her retrieve. The retrieve closes the circle. Hex relaxes, and in the act of retrieving, exhibits a playfulness reminiscent of her puppy days. After all these years of watching her be a hard-charging machine, I still find it surprising to watch her flash the bird like a trophy on the return. She carefully places the delicate ball of feathers in my hand with a gentleness so unlike the rigidity of her point. As part of our retrieval tradition, I hold the bird out to her, and after one final sniff, I give her a quick pat and a "Good girl." Then a repeat of "Hunt dead!" sets her off to do it all again. These actions unfold in fleeting moments, but coalesce into the strongest memories.

Chukars are called devil birds for lots of reasons, but they will always be a source of joy for me in real time and in memory. I have followed my dogs in pursuit of chukars over most of Eastern Oregon, a sizable portion of Idaho, a sliver of Washington, and a couple days' worth of Montana. I leave boot prints on the land that eventually weather away, but I also leave blood and sweat in these rocky, rugged places in trade for the wonderful memories I carry home.

My latest hunts have taken me to what might be the perfect place for walking hunters and rangy dogs—a place I can walk as far as my legs can carry me. It's a place where the hills are covered in short prairie grass that rolls and undulates in the wind, a wind that brings new smells with every change of direction. Here are the smells of rain coming in from late summer downpours brought by clouds that wander the sky, and the smells of cattle grazing fresh grass between the watering holes. But I'm here for the birds, and theirs is the smell Hex enjoys most. As the wind hits a momentary lull, it's time to move, because the clouds of mosquitoes start to gather. I turn my gaze down and release Hex from heel and we let the sun chase us across the prairie, marking our progress in points, flushes and retrieves.

This isn't our first trip across this landscape of long rolling hills and hidden coulees. No, that was years ago. Hex was in her first season, and I was green to the ways of the prairie birds. We made quite the pair, learning on the fly what made suitable habitat for sharptails, how to navigate all the new and wonderful smells, and how to dodge the cactus. Midway through that first trip we celebrated Hex's first birthday. Though I would like to claim that was the day she got her first sharptail, I honestly can't recall. I can say that trip, set the bar, defining how our hunts would play out in the years to come. I knew I was blessed with a dog that quickly adjusted to new species and ground, coming home a better bird dog with each unique experience.

It's such a joy to watch Hex cross this landscape. The poetry of movement is inherent in a veteran gun dog, and she eats up the miles with ease, cutting back and forth, head down about her business. I take this all in as she disappears and reappears over a ridge or out of a low spot, occasionally disappearing into the deeper shadows of a wild plum thicket when the sun moves behind some clouds. She reappears a little farther down the coulee in the sunlight, still eating up ground in search of birds.

A stutter step in the movement of my dog is the first clue that her intentions have changed. New alertness enters her body, evidenced by her tail. Over the years, I have learned two truths about Hex: if she is on point but her tail is moving, she is in the scent cone and the birds are moving away. Nine times out of ten, they have moved far enough that a relocate command will let her lock the birds down, giving me the best opportunity for a clean shot. Scenario two is a rock-solid tail, the only movement being the white hairs at the tip flagging in the wind. The birds on this point are locked down tight, and I'm on deck.

Again, the sight of my dog on a point will always be a favorite moment. It gives me that dopamine hit, gets the blood flowing and nudges my body into action. The gun is shifted, and my right hand rests on the grip, trigger finger outside the guard and thumb hovering over the safety. The rest of my body releases accumulated tension, and muscle memory takes over.

Closing the distance, I swing wide to Hex's right for an unobstructed view of the dog and field. Excitement, anticipation and calm all vie for dominance as I move in to flush.

Each step brings me closer to the explosion and completion of this task. My time to act is here, and the grouse start rising from the prairie. Wings scrape grass as they cup, clawing upward and weaving among their covey mates, trying to stay together while distancing the covey from danger.

I single out a bird from the mass of feathers and clucks and once again cede control to all I've experienced: the memory of every time I've looked at a flying target and pulled the trigger. Gun up, pointed, and the trigger pulled once, then twice, which is shorthand for a double. I get to send Hex rocketing through the grass for one retrieve, and then another. A smell of the bird, a pat, and a "Good girl" completes our ritual. Placing the birds in my vest, we head off over the rise in pursuit of the next flush. There are still plenty of miles and daylight left to explore these rolling prairies, making new memories in another wild place.

The journey started in the wild places of my youth, where my days were filled with adventures and dreams of hunting. And here, years later, I find myself in a new landscape, this a wide prairie instead of the tangled farms of my home country, the ragged crags of my chukar dreams.

Over the next ridge, perhaps birds, perhaps not, exploring, walking, just one more ridge into the unexpected. There's no way to tell where this road will take me, or where the end might lie. For that I am entirely grateful.

David Zoby
Grouse Magic

"How do you know but ev'ry Bird that cuts the airy way, Is an immense world of delight, clos'd by your sense five?" – William Blake

I always said, toeing a length of spruce into a campfire, that one season I was going to skip hunting elk and spend some weekends with my dogs hunting blue and ruffed grouse all over Wyoming. I said I'd fill a cooler with exotic foods—heirloom tomatoes from my friend's garden, smoked walleye, the prized cuts from last year's whitetail hunt in Kansas, and scores of beer and *brut* iced down to the max. I was going to teach the elk hunters a lesson on high culture and conspicuous leisure. Nobody questioned my sincerity, so I believed it myself. And yet, I never went. Instead, I marched into the unknown, crawling into drainages all over the West with the latest bow hunting devices and grotesque dehydrated foods. When blue grouse exploded beneath my boots, I paused, caught my breath, and moved on.

And so, it surprised me this year when I did what I always said I wanted to do: I eschewed elk hunting, loaded up my two Labs, Henderson and Rocket, and drove into the Sierra Madres with an idea of starting a new tradition—grouse camp.

With the recent passing of Jim Harrison and Anthony Bourdain, it seems like something should be done merely in the name of appetite, the vulgar world of excess. After all, who is left to live lavishly in the face of ruin? My one twenty-quart cooler was full of ice, varieties of craft beer, two magnum bottles of *brut*, and fixings to make deer-steak fajitas. I brought three types of cheese: Gouda, havarti, and a rare Gruyere. Navel oranges, homemade salsa, smoked sockeye, a loaf of zucchini/banana bread a neighbor gifted me. I bought three varieties of cured sausage, which I referred to generically as *dingus*. Dark chocolate, figs, and some cherries from British Columbia rounded out my trip into extravagance. I brought a copy of *Sunset* magazine for easy reading and fire-starter. There was no danger of starvation or boredom.

Not wanting to rush things, I stopped at the Hobo Pool at Saratoga, Wyoming, and soaked with a society of octogenarians who appreciated the finer things in life. One guy with a shocking white combover wore goggles and fins. He sculled along in the one hundred and nine-degree water. I had to sit on the lip of the pool with only my feet in the water. Someone mentioned a moose had been seen in town. We all agreed that this summer was a scorcher. There were no less than twenty-three private jets sitting on the tarmac just outside of town. One of the jets, it was noted, had a shower that could accommodate six at one time. Such observations introduce an awkwardness among strangers. So, we sat there for a while in silence. We said nostalgic things about the first days of fall. We said we wish for change.

It was a bummer that fires smudged the skies, but I persevered all the way to lunchtime, when I sauntered in flip-flops over to a passable pizza restaurant. I ate outside at one of the wrought iron tables, my dogs leashed and tied to a table leg. I could just make out the mountains through the haze. Both dogs panted heavily. Tourists, or what passes for tourists in Saratoga, went in and out of the antique shops along Main Street. They came out moments later empty-handed.

That afternoon I set my tent up near a stream. Cattle had pulverized the streambank and left evidence splattered all over, but they were off somewhere else now, chewing and regurgitating, chewing and regurgitating—the national pastime. We had the whole area to ourselves. I loaded my 20-gauge and began walking up the ridges where I saw dozens of grouse the year before. Hunting in shorts was a first for me. The dogs weren't sure what we were doing.

Walking through the alders and scrub oak was tough on the dogs, especially Rocket. They had been with me in Alaska all summer, at sea level. Now, on the flanks of steep mountains, they were all tongues and sweat. The scrub oak did a number on my bare legs. Henderson, the puppy, wheezed and lay down as if he couldn't go on. I had two thirty-two-ounce bottles of water, but the dogs were burning through it with no trouble. I decided to sit in the shade for an hour and press on when the shadows lengthened. I ate some *dingus* and wondered why I hadn't brought some spicy mustard with me. While we were sitting, I heard a bull elk bugle from a dense patch of trees. Another bull answered.

We scoured the places where I'd seen grouse the previous season, but there were none. Wouldn't you know it, the elk continued to bugle in forty-five-minute intervals, talking smack. It always seems, no matter how I plan things, my desires are always satisfied in the wrong manner. The sunset blazed crimson as we wandered back to the campsite. The idea of all that champagne made me pick my pace. The dogs sprinted forward and belly-flopped in the creek.

The sound of a plastic cork popping in the middle of the Medicine Bow National Forest is a sound I can get behind. I poured a huge tumbler of bubbly. I opened the cheeses and let Rocket have a big chunk of Havarti. He's 14 now —what can it hurt? Henderson didn't get any, and he fumed and paced over the injustice of it all. The champagne gave up its carbonation too soon, one of the characteristics of cheap booze. The stuff had all the grace of flat mineral water. I lit a stick fire and set up my gas stove.

The deer meat was messy and hard to contain in the tortilla. I ate most of it overly raw, as I had forgotten my head lamp. It was way past 10 o'clock when I crawled into the tent. The society of elk wandered across the same ridge where I had hunted for grouse all afternoon. I heard at least three different bulls claim the ridge as their own. By midnight it was getting ridiculous. The elk were getting out of hand. They were so close now that I could hear the gentle pleas of the cows, the mews of calves, and half-hearted bugles of spike elk that haven't yet learned to do it right. My dogs glowered through the mesh of the tent. Henderson growled. But the elk persisted. And so did the stars, scattered as they were above the carved black skyline of the Sierra Madres, like broken glass, like so many disconnected thoughts.

When I woke the next morning, most of the ice in my cooler had melted. The figs and cherries had freed themselves from their plastic bags and floated in the meltwater. The magnum of brut had capsized and emptied its contents into the icy water. Two formerly edible lengths of *dingus* had been submerged in the mixture of water and champagne and now were swollen to three times their original size. My stomach didn't feel steady. Sitting on the cooler, I ate an orange for breakfast, and drank one of those caffeinated energy drinks that don't taste right. I loaded my shotgun and pressed up the ridge to check once more for grouse.

***

My professor, the late Larry Levis, used to say that being a wild animal, say a wren or a raven, would contain more ecstasy in a single moment than a whole human life. He was riffing off Blake, and all the thousands of poets who came to the same conclusion: that nature is the only thing worth saving; animals are simply honest. Levis said we wouldn't be able to contain ourselves if we knew the pleasure of being a wild bird. There was no way to prove him wrong, so we let the idea fly around freely. In Richmond, Virginia, in 1994, how could you stop it? Some of my fellow grad students often holed up in dive bars in the Churchill Neighborhood of Richmond in hopes of getting a glimpse of him strolling along the darkened streets at ungodly hours. He lived in a dark house and wrote all that winter about birds, especially quail that slept in the vineyards in a California that no longer exists. His yard was bare dirt and the city pigeons dusted there in the afternoons. Did we see him? Did we ever get to encounter him and ask him about how he wrote his poems? Not very often. I was in my twenties, it felt okay to go home empty-handed. Failing seemed to be useful for the future, especially if you were planning on writing for a living.

But once I saw him in the wee hours, a slender man coming up Butler Street in an overcoat. His hands were in his pockets. That coat was all angles. The coattails were lightly brushing the snow, and he was, no doubt, thinking of flight.

This fall my appetite for grouse did not fade after a few extravagant trips into the public lands. I revisited old haunts where I usually find birds when hunting elk. I packed the cooler with ice, only to drain it after a few unproductive days of hunting grouse. Right where they had exploded from beneath my feet, there was nobody home. I ran into bow hunters who were unenthusiastic about my dogs, and even less so about my shotgun. I said to anyone who would listen that I'd be happy with one bird, thrilled with two. I put serious miles on my truck. My meals and eating habits withered. I ate at gas stations and truck stops. I skipped meals. I ate energy bars. I was learning that extravagance is only fun once or twice. By late September, I no longer packed a cooler with exotic foods. I lived, primarily, on pre-cooked grocery store chicken, tossing the obvious fat to the dogs. In the cab of my truck, a single Granny Smith apple rode along like a passenger. I put it in the cup holder. It never occurred to me to take a bite.

***

One can't exist on nostalgia alone. By October, the dogs were lean and anvil-headed. I hadn't fired a shot. I didn't know what to do next. My ombudsman, Kate O'Hara, was suffering from nostalgia too. She texted me one Saturday: *Just woke up. Let's go to the mountain with the dogs.*

At first, I thought it was a trap. She had edited several of my latest essays, and I worried that I had failed to pay her the going rate. I gathered only the necessary things: the shotgun and a handful of shells, the dogs, lip balm, a few Nalgene bottles half full of water. Gone were the days of overabundance and careful preparation. Besides, I thought we'd be back in town in time to go to Don Juan's for *posole*.

It snowed the night before, the first accumulation of the year. Above town, clouds settled over Casper Mountain like cream. I was gloomy. Kate was gloomy too. She recently won a prestigious writing award and now she was wondering if she could do it again, or if it was blind luck. I told her what Levis used to say: *When the river is full, we fish: when the river is empty, we stack stones.*

I'm not sure I know what that means. I told her about the pack of ravens Jim Harrison had befriended for the last twenty years of his life. They followed him on walks.

Our spirits lifted when the dogs went sprinting into the snowy woods, stopping here and there to evacuate themselves. But their movements were joy and power. Rocket shook off his years and bounded along with the puppy. The sun appeared in time to make the forest sparkle. Snow on the spruce needles smells better than any candle they sell at the mall. Here is the real thing, I thought, as we walked in silence. I walked with my gun broken open because I know she's afraid of loaded guns. Plus, it is a statement of panache that you don't see these days now that our heroes are dropping dead left and right. The dogs chased squirrels and finches. I told Kate that I wished I knew the names of the smallest finches that come through in the winter on their way south.

"One day I'm going to buy a book and try to learn their names," I said. "I'm an idiot on birds."

After an hour of walking, we found grouse tracks. They look just like pheasant tracks, only grouse wander more, as if they're not sure where they're going. They change their minds every ten feet. These grouse tracks swirled around the dripping spruce trees, and followed along the perimeters of aspen groves.

My dogs livened. Henderson's nose woke up a year ago and it's extraordinarily pleasant to watch him hone in on a bird. I was sure we'd find them. But no grouse flushed. The tracks dissolved into the woods. I didn't understand it. We moved on. Another hour down the trail and we were back into grouse tracks. These were so fresh I knew we were just behind the birds. I kept telling Kate that they were here, that we were going to see them soon. I snapped my gun together. The dogs were in top form, crashing the patches of wild currants, whirling in the sprigs of fallen aspen. But nothing. When we gave up, the first bird flushed straight up from Rocket's muzzle.

It was a large blue grouse, the slate-colored wings cutting powerfully as the bird shot up and up. Often, blue grouse will alight in a nearby tree and survey the area, but not this one. Its breast was speckled gray and white, and there was black in there too. The fan steered the bird, adjusting and angling, dividing the air. The bird twisted up and over one-hundred-foot-tall spruce trees. There was a stand of aspens between me and the bird, so I couldn't shoot. With the right angle, the fan cut the air and sailed the bird out over the wet forest.

Just as the first bird rocketed out of sight, another came up, this one right in front of Henderson. I raised my gun. It felt unnatural and unwieldy, like holding a length of firewood. I hadn't fired a gun in a year. I missed. But the next shot must have grazed the bird, for the wings redoubled their effort, yet the bird slowly sunk into spruce branches. His flight wobbled and took him veering into the wet boughs. He tumbled to the ground and Rocket was on him instantly. Two more birds flushed, but I was empty. Kate marked where one of the birds went. She thought maybe it landed in one of the tallest trees one hundred yards away.

We took the bird from Rocket and paused for a moment. We were both hungry. I had nothing in my pack, not even any dingus. We put the bird in the pack so that the fan peeked out.

"All I have is water," I said.

"I saw an apple in your truck," she said.

We looked around half-heartedly for the bird Kate marked, but I have mixed feelings about shooting blue grouse out of trees. (Shooting a grouse off a tree branch feels a bit like receiving a Valentine's card from your bank.) I've shot grouse off tree branches a few times, but I always end up apologizing to the universe afterwards. We didn't look too long. We were already talking about lunch. Kate said she didn't think it was right to shoot a grouse off a branch. My heroes have always been suckers for birds.

If we hurried, we could make it to Don Juan's before the dinner crowd. We cleaned the grouse at my truck. I had to dig around the cab for a knife. I had no plastic baggies for the carcass. The plan was to stuff the breasts with grilled pineapple and red onion. I'd wrap it in prosciutto and put it on the grill. Kate wanted to take the carcass and make wild bird stock in the theme of Jim Harrison. I collected enough snow to stuff in the body cavity for the trip down the mountain. She poured water on my hands and I rubbed them together to clean up. I asked Kate if she wanted the fan. People spread them out and dry them in their garages. But neither of us wanted to do that. So, I dropped the most perfect instrument of flight into a flurry of feathers at my feet. The fan twisted one more time as it felt the air, one final trick on its way down.

I told her about Levis and the way he talked about birds as if they were lost relationships.

"When I was at KU, I always wanted to have a professor like that. I went to their offices and tried to get them to mentor me, but they turned me down. They made me feel bad for asking."

We drove down the mountain, the washboards causing the truck to drift. On both sides of the truck was sky. For some reason, my mind clicked back to the fall of 1976, when my brother and I found some king daddy bottles of Miller High Life in the woods behind our house. Teenagers stashed their hard-fought victories in the strips of woods. We tied the bottles of beer by their necks with twine and dragged them behind our bikes through the neighborhood.

"And when they exploded," I told Kate, "they did it in style."

Shards of glass went everywhere, and there was the not-so-bad, wheaty scent of beer. I didn't drink back then, I told her. So, we just sort of huddled around the beer and smelled it before it soaked completely into the asphalt.

My truck rattled over the washboards as we descended. The aspens were at their peak, blazing like swaths of fire. In a week, the trees would be bare. We split the single apple as we went. It was what we had. It was small and sour. But I was surprised it had lasted as long as it did. It was enough to get us home.

Christine Peterson
A Lesson from the Bird Dog Who Turned Me into a Hunter

Tuco chased the rooster until it flew just high enough over the golden grass of the eastern Wyoming prairie for me to shoot. I threw up my gun, looking down the barrel at what would become my first bird: my first anything.

I waited. My young Labrador glanced back at me. I shot.

The pheasant dropped, and Tuco, not quite two years old, took off after it.

He carried it back to me, completing a loop between dog and human stretching thousands of years from when both species first realized they each had something to offer the other.

I said "good boy" too many times to count, then knelt with the iridescent rooster in one hand and made Tuco sit next to me. My husband, Josh, snapped a picture. In that instant, we both looked how we felt: proud, and maybe a little surprised that he flushed a bird and I shot it.

For that fleeting moment, we were just...there.

Then we stood again. He raced off with his nose to the ground, and I shoved the bird in my vest. We went back to looking for what's next, anticipating the next smell, the next flush, the next opportunity.

The whole exchange took no more than a few minutes, from flush to photo finish. But it was the culmination of half a decade of me contemplating hunting, writing about hunting, talking to people about hunting, and even practicing hunting. It was the nearly two years Josh and I spent training Tuco, even though we didn't know what we were doing and he didn't know what he was doing. It was the culmination of the three of us embracing our youth and naivete and bumbling through it all.

I should have known that moment's significance eight years ago. I should have known what it could teach me and what he could teach me. But I didn't. Not yet.

Made for each other

All I wanted was a dog. It didn't matter what kind of dog. I grew up with a one hundred forty-pound malamute who slept on my bed until he was too old to climb all the way up. A Siberian husky outran me through high school until her heart gave out sometime after she turned 17.

I didn't just want a dog. I needed a dog. Because here's the thing: I was, and am, that dog person. I worked long, lonely hours by myself from home. I had started a strange habit of staring out my window and sprinting outside to pet any dogs who walked by—acceptable behavior in a child, odd in an adult.

But there are good times to get dogs and bad times to get dogs. Living with my parents for six months while my new husband finished school was not a good time. So for Christmas, Josh gave me a puppy-a-day calendar. They were all Labradors—yellow, black, chocolate, silver—and instead of laughing at the funny joke, I cried. I really needed a dog, and now everyone staring at me sobing over a calendar surrounded by torn wrapping paper knew just how much. Soon after, my mom told me about her friend who had Labrador puppies. We should look at them, she said. I called the friend within minutes and went over that afternoon. Six long weeks later, there we were, sitting downstairs in his living room with a little yellow ball of fur curled under the crook of my knees. This one ran over to me to seek refuge from his siblings. He and I both knew: he would be ours.

Tuco and I grew up together like everyone does with their first dog. We moved to a new town and figured out where to find pheasants. He was my refuge from bad bosses and my solace through loneliness and depression. Even by the time he was fully grown at ninety pounds, Tuco let me pick him up and hold him in my lap. When the temperature fell to twenty below zero and the furnace went out in our run-down rental, Tuco kept me warm as I typed away on the floor with my back pressed up against his. The three of us settled in yet another new house. We learned how to find grouse in the snow.

But those joys came with an unexpected price. It's the one all of us face when we give our hearts to dogs. One day, they'll be gone. So on a hot summer day while we were lying on the cold tile floor, we agreed that he'd live forever. I made him promise. And time went on.

Josh and I had a daughter. Tuco's face turned white. Then we moved again, taking him and that little girl to another town. He pretended she was an inconvenience, but he still curled up by her bed each night. Everywhere we went, he and I ran, miles and miles and miles. He kept in shape for bird season, I kept the demons at bay, and we learned a little bit more about what we were supposed to be doing.

That's what you do with your first dog. You teach them. But really, they're just teaching you.

Then last year, Tuco started drinking more water than usual. Lots of water. I wondered if he had a kidney problem or diabetes. He'll be fine, I told myself before I found out he wouldn't be fine. The veterinarian walked into the room and told me that the 8-year-old Labrador who turned me into a hunter had blood cancer.

She told me he'd have a couple months, maybe longer. We should make him comfortable. She told me there were treatments, but multiple myeloma was a rare disease and the prognosis uncertain. I couldn't stop crying.

I wanted to ask questions. I'm a journalist. That's how I make sense of the world. But I couldn't ask the vet anything just yet. Instead, I talked to Tuco. I just kept telling him it would be alright, as though he needed my reassurances.

I didn't know what to do, so we went for a run.

Then I made more phone calls, got more tests, and decided to try treatment. When I finally ran out of questions, we went hunting.

We have what we need

Weeks later, chemo and steroids coursing through his veins, we pulled up behind a truck parked in the cured grass and sagebrush of Wyoming. I opened the door and lifted Tuco out. Two dogs jumped out of the other truck. Their white faces all looked the same.

It was a meeting I'd been anticipating for eight years: Tuco would finally hunt with his mom and sister. His mom was 13. His sister was eight, just like him. Moments later, they took off. They had birds to find.

Noses to the ground, they busted through thick, lanky willows and tall grasses, flushing roosters and bringing them back. The dogs hunted as if no one was sick. No one was old.

I watched him, and I thought. Maybe the drugs will work. Maybe he'll be the exception. Maybe I'll have him for longer than anyone thinks. Maybe we'll still hunt those chukar next month, go on that backpacking trip next June. Maybe he'll make it to another hunting season.

Then I stopped myself. Waiting for what's next wasn't ever the point.

I spent his whole life hoping for more. Just one more nap, one more run, one more hunt. All the while I had, right then, the very things I was longing for. And even if he went into remission, if he made it to our chukar hunt, and even the next bird season, we would still, one day, run out of time. A life spent together with a dog like Tuco isn't about what's next, it's about what's now.

So I stopped wondering and just watched him in the willows, tail whipping back and forth. I should have known with that first bird, in that moment we sat by each other with pride, that all he'd been trying to do was teach me to trust him, to trust us. And, perhaps most importantly, to quit worrying so damn much.

Chad Love
Absolution in Four Acts

September

I am the only person here. It's just the dogs and me and the wind and melancholy and that feeling of being so perfectly alone, like you're the last person on earth and don't really mind.

I unload the truck, set up the tent, feed the dogs, then make myself a gin and tonic and sit at the picnic table.

I listen to the rhythm of the wind and wonder at the passage of years. I think about regrets and words better left unsaid; anger best kept bottled up. And I think about joy, too, and happiness. I experienced a lot of both here, but I wonder if I should have come, knowing this spot was not mine alone.

The hesitation was real, and I almost didn't load up and make the drive. I considered going back to the mountains for dusky grouse instead.

Because there's something missing here, in the place and in the moment; something I once thought essential to me. And there's sadness here, too; the kind of wistful sadness that causes you to dwell on things more than you should.

But I came anyway. Because that's what September is for: birds and dogs and pondering and confronting bittersweet memory. September is wind and loneliness and waning sun and a long walk in a lonely place. It's the first whisper of autumn in that dusky twilight between summer and fall, light and dark, heat and cold.

But this evening, it's for coming to terms with the past and looking toward the future. Or trying to, anyway. It's hard to let the past be the past, because the past will never offer you the same terms. It's here to stay. The past occupies the present just as surely as we do.

To think otherwise, to try to shove all that made you into some dark corner of your mind labeled "Past: Do not open and do not dwell" is folly, doomed to failure. It's what people tell themselves when they're trying to run from something to which they will always be tethered. I've been guilty of it more times than I care to admit, and will surely do so in the future. Because we can never wipe the slate clean. Life is indelible. It etches, deeply.

I think about that for a bit, look into the bottom of my cup, and make another drink.

After dinner, I put the dogs back in the box, grab a bottle, and take a walk into the darkness. It's time to ring in the seasonal New Year.

January 1st doesn't mean a damn thing to me. Never did. Just another day where the cheap booze and cheaper nostalgia of the night before finally wears off and you realize through the fog of a hangover that not a goddamned thing has changed in your world or anyone else's.

If you really want to hear the world creak and groan and slip from one epoch into the next, walk out into the prairie on the first night of September. Find a hill to sit on, turn your face up to the sky, let that ancient celestial light strike your eyes, and listen to the ancient gods whispering in your soul's ear: old thoughts, old yearnings, old fears, old hopes, all welling back up from within on the tendrils of that first, softly-keening fall breeze that marks the trembling of the seasons and the dimming of the summer light.

Those stirring gods will tell you that despite our skin and bones and blood and the wounds we inflict on each other and the land, we humans are ephemeral, temporary. And when we are gone, and what we think is so important, so pressing, so urgent and so righteous is gone as well: all of our furious certainty and rage will mean nothing, be nothing.

Sitting there in the elegiac twilight and the rustling wind of passage and change, I make my resolutions for the next seasonal year, and my peace with the lessons I've learned over the one just past. Some of those lessons came dearly and wounded deeply, as a certain kind of learning and the clarity that pain provides always will. But it taught me, too, because darkness is as much a gift as light, if you choose to learn from it.

Sometime long past midnight, the gods stop talking to me, so I stumble back to camp and fall into my sleeping bag, dreaming of sharptails and early fall thunderstorms lighting up the night sky.

The next morning I wake, make coffee and go ghost hunting. It feels strange to be here with only my own thoughts, my own dogs, my own voice. But life goes on, and sometimes friendships don't, so I tromp the sandhills alone behind an old setter who knows the prairie grouse game well, and a young pointer who doesn't.

I walk about a fair bit along routes I vaguely recognize from years past. Leo, the old setter, points a single prairie chicken, which I shoot, then Abbey busts a group of sharptails, which I shoot at but shouldn't. She'll learn eventually. I'm not so sure about myself.

I meander, wool-gather, remember, and occasionally shoot a bird. I revisit some places I recognize, find some spots that still hold the after-image of moment and memory, and have conversations with some old, rapidly-fading ghosts. Leo finds another chicken, because that's what he does, and Abbey redeems herself on her first pointed sharptail.

It is a wordless, wonderful morning. I came here looking for closure, a measure of solace and atonement for mistakes made and regrets for things said. But I discover what I once thought essential—isn't—in fact it never really was, and that I may hurt, but I will be alright. And that's a damn good thing to finally realize about yourself when you've been swimming around in the crucible of doubt and anger just waiting to melt.

I find, meandering out there in the grass, that I don't melt so easily. And that if you walk far enough toward the event horizon that always hovers in front of you, what melts away is not you, but the weight of what others think of you.

That night I celebrate, make a fire, cook the sharptail and split it with the dogs, and as the flames dance, I ponder absolution. Absolution from sins, flaws, guilt, anger, resentment, bitterness, pettiness; all the things that make us human right along with the good, all washed away in the moment.

That's what a good long walk behind fast dogs will do for you. It's temporary, of course. What we are always comes back to us.

But right now, I'll take temporary and be damn happy to have it, here in the silence of a lonely camp and a waning moon.

On nights like this, when I teeter half in and half out of the darkness, I wonder how much longer I'll be doing this: fleeing into the dusky twilight leaf-rustling autumn, alone, when feelings usually held close to the bone and soul come up for air. And tonight, in the last dying breath of evening, I'm missing a memory and a friend now gone. But there are no u-turns, no do-overs, no nostalgia-tinged rationalizations for things said and done, no matter how badly the head and the heart want them. You choose your road, and then you don't look back, because absolution only goes so far.

October

It adds up.

Every sweat-soaked mile walked, every ancient Cretaceous hill climbed, every bur pulled from a dog's pad, every horizon-spanning sea of grass crossed, every bone-jarring, dust-choked county section of road driven, every desiccating blast-furnace wind faced, every wild, out-of-range flush, every heartbreaking miss, every stupid mistake, every bit of bad judgment and every stroke of bad luck. It all adds up. Call it prairie grouse math.

The glaring, utterly inescapable sun will beat down on your head as you walk mile after endless mile in search of a bird more apparition than solid form. You'll top crumbling, fossil-encrusted ridges that were once part of an ancient inland sea, and you'll stare off to a distant horizon across what is now a waving, largely unpeopled sea of grass, and you'll despair of ever finding a bird in all that silent, implacable vastness.

And when you do find the birds, when the faint scent of game finally wafts across your dog's nose, more often than not the birds will flush out of range, aloft and untouchable on that ever-blowing plains wind, leaving you standing there sweating, swearing, and wondering why the hell you ever agreed to do this.

And then you'll go back to camp, exhausted, and peel yourself out of sweat-and-dust-encrusted clothing that still carries the faint scent of countless steps through prairie grass. You'll try to cool down, recover, grab a beer and cook dinner, try to remember the last time a damn bird so squarely kicked you in the teeth.

You'll go to bed to the sound of the wind, always the wind, rustling through the branches of the gnarled old prairie cottonwood you're camped under, and you'll wake up before the sun, make coffee on the campstove, load up the dogs, and go do it all over again.

November

There's a rusty old gate in an overgrown parking area perched high atop a windswept prairie hill, on a half-forgotten expanse of public land near where I once lived and had a life, a long time ago.

To get to the land beyond, and the few quail it holds in the even fewer decent bird years this hard, capricious land offers, you must open that gate and step through into the world beyond.

But you must mind what you bring with you when you step through. It's a long walk down, and an even longer walk out. I read once that people see in the world what they carry in their hearts. Carry too little into that country, and you'll never reach where you're trying to get to. Carry too much, and you'll never make it back to where you started.

It's damn hard land, and as I wander across it, I think about the people who once tried to sink the roots of a life into this place and turn it into something it never should have been.

It seems like folly now, of course, with the gift of hindsight and dust-borne history to help pass judgment, but back then they were just poor, desperate, hardscrabble folks with dreams of a new life and a place to call their own. My people.

The heart wants what it wants, regardless of reason or logic or reality. Someone wanted a home here, once. Their hearts said yes. The land said otherwise. Such is the human condition, in most things of love, land and life, and such it will always be.

In the end we're all itinerant ghosts, following hearts that often lead us astray.

Some of us weather the storms that invariably buffet those decisions, and some do not. And some of us are smart enough to follow dogs rather than hearts.

These days, I tend to follow dogs and birds, leaving matters of the heart to others who can better bear the wounds.

Only the wind and a few quail call this place their own now; tough survivor birds finding a way to hang on out here on the ragged edge of their respective ranges, the scaled quail from the West and the bobs from the East as they mingle in the transition zone between two worlds.

I may find a few birds, or I may not. But I'll find beauty and solitude. I'll find lonely ghosts still haunting the exposed bones of their own tragic history, and I'll briefly connect once again with that intrinsic, unknowable something that compels some of us to seek our answers in the abandoned and forgotten corners of life where others rarely visit.

We chase birds and dogs and solace because we're all wounded on some level, and places like this stop the bleeding, if only for a little while.

On my way out, I stop and pick up an old box turtle shell. I've always had a knack for finding these old shells, and I would throw them in my vest and give them to a friend who loved turtles but never could seem to find a shell of her own. I once told that same friend that trust is a safe deposit box for our soul's secrets.

But we no longer share either turtle shells or secrets. That friend moved on and so did I, so I admire its sun-bleached dignity for a moment, then set it back down for the grass and wind and time to claim as their own.

I walk away with the past on my mind, and I am reminded that wind sighing through winter grass is the most achingly lonely sound I know. Except for the word "goodbye," spoken for the last time.

December

I am sitting on the tailgate in the waning of a cold, brief December afternoon, stroking an old dog's head. It has been a long day of hunting and not much shooting, and we are both exhausted. I haven't done him any favors today with my shooting, and yet he looks up at me, and what I see in his eyes is acceptance. Pure, unadulterated acceptance.

After all the shit I sometimes give him, he accepts me, unconditionally, with all my flaws and warts and deficiencies and failings.

Dogs do that. Most people don't. That's why I love dogs.

It seems that so many of us try to reinvent ourselves—at least in our own minds—over and over again. We follow the self-styled self-help gurus, always chasing a version of ourselves that simply doesn't exist.

I've always known who I am. I couldn't reinvent myself—I actually have a few times—and failed spectacularly.

I am a difficult person. I'm stubborn, argumentative, judgmental, proud, often distrustful, overbearing, aloof, and distant. Quick to take offense, quick to argue, quick to fight. I can be ugly and unpleasant and selfish and petty.

Because I'm human.

But I've got a few good qualities, too, buried somewhere down amongst the bad, and if there's anything I've learned from dogs, it's that really knowing yourself doesn't have a damn thing to do with getting advice from strangers; it comes from holding on to the ones who know you—even the bad you—and who are willing to hold on to you in return. If you want to find out who you truly are, then find people who absolve you—with all your complications and complexities—the way your dog does; without judgment and without conditions.

But that's a damn rare thing, which is why I generally prefer dogs.

So I guess the one piece of life advice I feel qualified to give is this: Just stick with dogs.

It works for me.

Reid Bryant
Gestures of Intent

For the first few years of my adulthood I lived on a ridgetop farm in central Massachusetts. The pastures and woodlots that I called home flanked a few miles of rutted dirt road, and in the encompassed acres I hunted grouse, woodcock, and pheasants. I did so typically in the frost of early mornings and the slanting sun of afternoons, around the edges of the milking schedule. I did my hunting largely alone, save for the company of a cocky little American Brittany, whose work was my play. He had little regard for cows.

These were the early years of a hunter's life, wherein the frivolity of youth was giving way to a family and a job that took precedent. In turn, I hunted around the edges of the day. Too often these edges were only fractions of an hour, but they nonetheless were mine. I even managed at times to find a bird or two.

On one such morning, in the tangled corner behind the Blackmers' dairy barn, I dumped a male woodcock just as the sun was cresting the far ridge. Being late for chores, I picked up the little body with its matchstick legs, smoothed back the feathers and admired my prize with the mixture of joy and mild regret that I hold for woodcock in particular. But with the sun rising higher and the day getting late, I tucked the bird into my game bag, whistled up the dog, and hustled back out of the covert to the truck. I scooted up the road to the home farm, pulled into the barnyard, and got out, shucking off my chaps and my whistle and taking the collar off my dog. I threw the vest in a corner of the woodshop where its contained treasure would remain cool and safe until the day's end. I then went off to see after a row of hungry Jersey cows, none of whom were too pleased with my tardiness.

I worked a full day in the October fields, pushing manure into windrows and pulling buckthorn out of stone walls. I ate dinner at the farm, and only when the stars were high did I return to the woodshed to pluck and clean my little bird. I opened the game bag to see the interior fabric painted with stark white droppings, the distressed leavings of a bird I'd assumed long dead; the woodcock had, it turned out, only been wounded. That bird had, at my hand, suffered the indignity of a day spent pierced and clinging to this world, undoubtedly in pain.

It slipped away slowly in the back of my vest. All of this on account of my haste.

I am not proud of this story. Truth be told, it is among the stories that I am least proud of in life, and it is not one I tell often or easily. It does, however, illustrate a pointed lesson that I as a hunter assumed I had learned long before. I suppose, in retrospect, I had become somewhat complacent with the responsibility inherent in my role: as a hunter I had set out to kill things, and that morning I had failed to do so with intention and with certainty. Perhaps what shames me most is that I had failed to give a lovely creature and a lovely morning its due.

This story, I hope anyway, illustrates a philosophical conundrum that I find central to all hunting. I love these things I seek to kill, though I both protect and harm them, and feel a little bit sad about my compulsions. I don't know why this is. I do know, however, that an education in hunting is an education in purpose. It is also an education in absolutes. Perhaps this is what I stand to learn most through my journey into the uplands. I know that, in my case anyway, hunting has forced me to lean into nature's questions and nature's uncomfortable answers; it has shared teachings about finality, and taking responsibility for what I can't undo, what I can't put back. Hunting is not a catch-and-release sport.

It is no mystery that bird hunting, when done to success, removes a bit of flesh and feather from the living landscape. Hunting cannot easily exist independent of killing, and that distinction should be clear. My hunting is more than a lovely walk in the woods with a fine old gun; it is by definition an anticipatory action, done with intention. When followed through, it encompasses snuffing out things that were once vibrant and alive, plain and simple. I was not raised a hunter, and as I began to identify as such, I began to see myself as a different creature altogether than the one I'd been before: being a hunter required of me conviction, and the inevitable reality that my hands would get bloody, and the creatures that I loved would die.

So where do we go with this conversation? The answer is too personal to address in specifics, but from a spiritual or philosophical standpoint, I'd venture that the shame I felt in leaving that bird to suffer has remained, cropping up at points when the pressures of time or daylight or my own distraction come to call.

I suppose that in those moments, a long-felt shame serves to remind me that in being an upland hunter, I cannot forget to thank the birds that allow me that identity. This simple gesture, offered humbly, may seem of no great cost or consequence…but perhaps it holds the most consequence of all.

Greg McReynolds
Time Collection

I wear a whistle for a spaniel, an Acme 210.5. Doug gave it to me sometime in the mid, 80s at the ending of an annual pilgrimage I took as a child, leaving south Texas at the end of the school year and spending summers with my grandparents in the rural north of England.

It was one of those long summer evenings above the fifty-third parallel where dog-training sessions could run late into the lingering twilight. We were standing in the gravel drive in front of the farm's old stone stables, long-ago converted to storage for more modern items like cattle feed and a Ford model A pickup with a worn-timber flatbed. Doug handed me a little box with the whistle inside.

"For your own dog," he said.

Even now, it is hard to explain how badly I wanted a gundog. I grew up on the gulf coast in the arid plain that was once tall-grass prairie when the bison were roaming. Now, it's fenced and grazed by Angus and Charolais cattle, except in the places where it is high-fenced and grazed by axis deer and hatchery-bred whitetail clones. We had border collies, and one in particular who was my constant companion, but they weren't gun dogs. I spent years circling ads, reading magazines and calling breeders whose pups I could not afford. I was despondent in my yearning for a dog, feeling like it would never come.

There was a long period of coming to terms with the reality of place as well. England is a place where I shot wood pigeons and rabbits, but I never hunted upland birds. Those were reserved for other people. Even Doug spent many more hours "driving" birds or "picking up" than he did shooting upland birds. In Texas, there was an even more defined class system that separated me from the landowners and leases big enough to hold huntable populations of bobwhite. I was well into my teens before a driver's license and liberal parents led to the realization that a whole world of public lands existed where no one could chase me off or look down on me.

The child's longing that stretched into the eons of youth are condensed into a few moments of despair. Crying myself to sleep over three strands of barbed wire strung across a creek that kept me from launching my canoe. The bitter disappointment when we were priced out of our small hunting lease. The dogs and hunts since then loom as larger memories of highs and lows, decades scribbled into synapse shorthand. A springer walking at heel through a high-school hallway en route to a science class. A Brittany pointing a covey of a bobwhite quail next to an impossibly tall patch of prickly pear cactus. A setter chasing a covey of Gambel's quail over the horizon.

Time moves along, but it doesn't disappear. It gathers up. Consolidates. Boils down to the best bits. And the worst.

Doug and his wife Audrey were generous in the North Yorkshire way that was symbolic of their generation. They were too young to have fought in the war, but old enough to have lived through it and be profoundly impacted by the years that followed. To this day, Audrey is a person who checks on people. She calls and writes, drops in, brings a cake or a newspaper. When we were children, she was always up for a day out with us. She was a wonderful friend to my grandparents, especially in their later years, as old age isolated them.

In the years I knew them best, they were empty nesters with their own children moved on and their grandchildren not yet arrived. Over a dozen or so years, Doug and Audrey gave me a Swiss army knife, lots of books, and a lasting love of gundogs that transcends hunting. Of the objects, it's the whistle that I hold closest.

Doug taught me to shoot wood pigeons with a well-worn FN Auto-Five. It was an ancient gun with a straight stock and short chambers. Three decades and many guns bought and sold since, I can still trace my preference to shotgun configuration to that specific gun. We rode in Doug's car as Sam the Labrador tried to climb into the front passenger seat I was riding in—his usual spot. I traced the "FN" on the butt plate with my index finger. Doug dropped me off at the end of a tree row that he had helped plant as a young man.

He and Sam drove to the other end and walked through, pushing roosted wood pigeons out and over my head. I stood waiting, a gamebag of cartridges at my feet because the belt was too big to buckle round my waist. They came over high and fast. I didn't even shoot at the first few. When I got over my hesitation, I felt the slow, pushy recoil of the A5, accentuated by the low-recoil, short shells.

"Well, did you hit any?" asked Doug jovially as he and Sam appeared through the trees. Sam quartered across the pasture, picking up the birds I had knocked down and bringing them to hand.

My current springer is likely the last in a line of spaniels for me, supplanted by setters a decade ago. She's long past retirement, 15 years old, sleeping away her days concerned by little besides a warm and comfortable place to snore.

The 210.5 hangs from a piece a paracord, the original lanyard and a subsequent replacement worn and gone. My two setters run big, and if I'm honest, the youngest one runs a bit wild, even for a fleet-footed hunter. A deeper, longer carry whistle has been in order for some time, but I haven't made the switch yet. Some of the delay has to do with my general resistance to change. And some has to do with that whistle being a touchstone to a very specific summer and the love of a dog so sincere that even now, I can close my eyes and feel my heart swell.

I was about ten years old at the time, and I'd spent a summer's worth of long evenings in Yorkshire helping Doug train a springer pup named Sally. A 10-year-old can love a puppy with every part of themselves. Doug was a serious trainer with high expectations for dogs. He'd always had labs, and he gave me endless grief for my unbridled love of Sally.

Eventually, her training ended, and the spaniel moved on to her new owners. In the meantime, Doug taught me to shoot rabbits and how to trap stoats and weasels. I learned to skin rabbits at lightning speed. And always, there were dogs. They were compact British-style Labradors, pups and professionals. And there was Sam, the yellow lab pup with a big blocky head with a penchant for digging, probably encouraged by the occasional day of ferreting for rabbits. He had that hard-headed, good-natured, can-do attitude that defines hunting labs. As a young dog, Sam once tried to "retrieve" a 12-bore superposed. Luckily, Doug wasn't one to worry too much about a few tooth marks in a gunstock.

A few years later, in a gift from the universe or a god who loves bird dogs and small boys, my grandparents retired and left the farm, buying a house next door to Sally the springer. I spent many summers with that springer and the others in her pack. Every day I would check in on the springers, throwing dummies or taking them for a run or just enjoying their company. I went to bed smelling of spaniels and dreaming of gundogs.

Years later, his knees gone and his mobility impaired, Doug acquired what turned out to be his last pup, a springer with a deformed leg that he took as a charity case with the beneficiary undetermined. Turned out Doug loved spaniels too, though I suppose we both knew that all along.

The man who taught me my earliest lessons in dog training is five years gone. Doug was my friend. He was a mentor. He had a strong handshake and a love of dogs that was much greater than his love of shooting. Doug had a broad Yorkshire accent and a laugh that came easily.

The dogs he left behind, remnants of a lifetime of dogs, have passed on as well. My own yearning for a pup was fulfilled by a springer at 15, and a long list of dogs since.

On a long ridge dotted with Gambel oak, century plant looms on a steep western hillside and a dry arroyo stretches out below. The land is public, the birds are wild and the dog is running to perfection. I wish Doug was here to see this foreign land, these desert birds and mostly the little dog, working like an engine.

Time moves on, consolidating into memory a few synapses, pieces of the past lingering in my brain. The setter rockets in a massive figure eight, stretching three hundred yards out, far beyond the reach of a spaniel whistle.

The moment passes, but it does not disappear.

Thomas Reed
The Last Chicken

"SG/08"

It had been there a long time, that package. I had seen it the same way you see something everyday that you don't really see at all. Like the same tree in the same front yard on different days, day-after-day-after-day. Walk by it. Know it's there. Don't even see it. Like that. I had pawed past it, moved it aside from other coded frozen packages with other ciphers. Packages of elk steak and burger, whitetail tenderloin. Nevada chukar. Huns. The whole feathered carcass of the rooster pheasant that I was saving for training the bird dog pup that had not even been born yet. Always found something else to cook up. Like elk steak, like that buck loin. Never "SG/08."

And yet here it is now, in my hand. Cold. Frozen. Old. Probably freezer-burned to shit. I don't even know why I picked it up....

But on this late summer afternoon, the package rests in my palm, the warmth of my hand melting the frost on the plastic, a hand print around a frozen hunk of water that protects—in theory—a chunk of meat from freezer burn. Even years later. A half decade later. Maybe. And I pull it out and take it to the kitchen sink and I turn the tap on hot and fill up the sink and begin the thaw.

In the steam of hot water hitting ice. It starts there. Flowing up and out. Duane asked me down to hunt for a few days. He would be there anyway, on the toe of the Wind River Range, set back against a slope of sagebrush, the vast open of the Great Divide Basin, once an inland ocean of saltwater, now a sea of salt-brush and sage, stretching south and east and west. Backs to the mountains. The Hyde family reunion would be wrapping up. A hunting family reunion. A hunting family's reunion. It was a tradition that had gone on and on and on. No picnics and flag football games. Just travel trailers parked in the middle of the sagebrush ocean, the Winds wearing a fresh skin of new snow, and the Hyde clan threading out in all directions carrying shotguns.

"Come down on the tail end of it," said Duane.

So I did. I would stay in Duane's trailer. I had three good setters, a young one coming and two in their prime. Duane, two Brits and a setter of his own.

I found the trailer standing all alone, the reunion over, the myriad Hydes scattered home. Just Duane and his dogs. No problem getting there. Good directions, but getting too dark to hunt that day, so we talked for a bit and ate some supper and talked some more and I curled up in one of the bunks. Tomorrow we would drift into the horizon on the rolling green-gray ocean. *Artemisia tridentata,* Wyoming big sage . . . .

***

The ice in the freezer bag melts now, the steam still rising, and I start to see the meat, as red-purple as coulee chokecherry in autumn leaf. Doesn't look too badly freezer burned.

They have been a part of my life for as long as I have carried a shotgun. When I was a young editor of a newspaper in the heart of southwestern Colorado, I shot piles of them, bouncing my old F-100 up a two track, carrying my Browning 12, following my mutt JD in hot pursuit. We had a mountain east of town that was all ours, and we hunted in the grayness of it nearpatches of yellowing aspen shedding leaves into September wind. JD was the bastard daughter of a spaniel mother and a black lab father, and she could hunt.

My friend Jack from college came out one year, and we each shot limits and then drove home to a town that now shares the same name as that grouse subspecies. We ate them over aspen coals on the backyard fire pit, pulling flannel and wool on against the high cold. It seemed then like it would never end: an icon bird in an icon landscape. More Western than the Marlboro Man. A hunt of felt Stetsons and straw Resistols, no ball caps. Pearl snaps. Wrangler jeans, pockets showing chew can circles. More Western than Theodore Roosevelt or John Wayne. An experience of open skies and good friends and Coors beer when it was still a regional beverage, when we drove vehicles that weren't made in Korea or Mexico. Just living life. Not taking things for granted, but perhaps not understanding that things ebb and flow, change and quit. Fade and flower. Die.

That morning Duane shared the land with me. It was his place. Had been his place, his family's place, year after year after year. Sure, it was public land, but it felt like it had another stamp—a generational one. I felt honored. Deeply.

We set out in different directions. Duane and Duke the setter going one way. Me with my entire pack another. I walked and followed. A light breeze came off the ocean into canine noses, and I followed some more. Walking. Always walking, the sun warm now, the dogs panting and threading their way west then east then south then back west, but always into the wind. Pulled by it. Beckoned by it, really. Coming back to get watered, then bursting out into it again.

Then Ike, the older, went on point and Sage backed and I whoa'ed up the pup, Echo, and it was there: three good dogs all pointing and the birds went up wild and out of range, but there was a straggler, and my gun swung and barked and then it was in my hand. Smelling of sagebrush and soil in a land of horny toads and cactus. An antelope buck barked at us from a rise, then took off. The dust from his hooves skeined into the wide.

We walked some more, and sometimes I talked to the dogs or whistled to the pup. But mostly, I followed. Quiet. It felt not right to yell or whistle there. There would be no outbursts in church. The dogs knew what they were doing anyway. An hour or two into the hunt, I heard the faint bark of Duane's shotgun off over a breaker of sage.

***

The bird is thawed enough now, and I find a filet knife and bend to the work, threading thick red muscle from hollow bone, breast meat and thigh meat. My hands are cold. The ice is barely out of the flesh. I dice it into chunks, cubes an inch thick. Then I work on the marinade, improvising. Soy sauce. Vinegar. Chipotle chili powder from Hatch. Pepper. Olive oil. Mix it all up. The meat goes into the marinade and into the refrigerator.

I started to hunt them with pointing dogs the year I lived in that Colorado mountain town. Not my pointing dogs. JD was a good dog, a working poor man's bird dog. A flusher. But not a true bird dog. My friend Jim had two setters, and when I went with him, which was more and more often, JD stayed home. She wasn't happy, but I had my reasons, and mostly they had to do with the romance of it all. Hard to imagine anything more handsome than a big male setter pointing a bird at the edge of an aspen grove with the flanks of a fourteen-thousand-foot peak in the distance. Jim turned me on to that. A life-changer for a young man with that gleam and that dream. We took horses sometimes, following the dogs up a mountain called Flat-Top north of town. The dogs drank up the country and we followed on horseback and the shotguns talked. Good living.

***

Throughout the afternoon, I check the bird, flipping the chunks over in the marinade, then start on the wood for the outdoor grill. My guest will be here before long, but for now there is only me and old setters sprawled loose on the porch.

By noon that day, I was circling back, the shine of the truck still far distant. I watched for Duane and then finally saw him, saw the puff of white setter zipping across the landscape far to the front, circling back, then running out again. Watched it from a mile away. Watched it some more, and then the dog stopped and I saw Duane shoot, then heard the shot. We walked parallel paths now, Duane and Duke down in a small valley, me on a ridge. I watched my dogs, two birds in the vest. Content. Mostly I watched Duane, watched man and dog sweep up a country.

We met at the truck and he smiled in that tired quiet way of his and said he had two birds too and said, "Duke's a younger man's dog."

He wiped sweat from the band of his Stetson with a handkerchief and put it back on, and we sat on the tailgate for a while, drank a Gatorade. Did not talk much, just listened. Listened to the sound of the mountain and the sage ocean, four dogs panting in concert in the shade of the Chevy.

"Well, we better clean these birds."

In the evening, I skewer chunks of meat out of the marinade onto kabobs, alternating wedges of onion and pepper and mushroom. My guest tonight is an old friend who enjoys wild game and good wine, and she pulls a cork while I go to get the coals ready. Alder from down on my creek for smoke, cottonwood to get it going. We don't talk much, and mostly that's my fault, because I'm off there.

Over the years, I moved north and chased JD after more birds in Wyoming on a stream named Muddy. Not a creek, really. Just a dry arroyo that was mostly caliche and greasewood. We found plenty of birds there, though, and shot them out of the sky and camped out there on the hardpan, drinking whiskey and clean air. It was a place where antelope barked from skylines and badgers hissed at your bird dogs as you hiked by and at night you laid under the stars and watched your breath steam away. The hunting and the hunt was indelible. Always took home a limit, nine in possession, three per day.

I moved north again and hunted those birds again, this time with a setter of my own I named Huntin' Hank and followed on a horse I called Ace. Hank swallowed the wind and the birds had no way of hiding from that kind of power. Talent. My shotgun barked and the horse always stood for me to mount again, then horse and dog and man moved off into the breeze, looking for more of the same. Once, I walked with a young lady who made me forget about birds and guns and horses. For a time. A few hours anyway. We talked and walked across that landscape, then missed Hank. I'd forgotten about working the dog. Found him. On point. Eight or nine hundred yards away. Holding. I apologized and laughed, and started to run and it took me what seemed like fifteen minutes to cover the ground at a sprint and when I got there, the dog still held until I said, "Okay, Hank," and he broke, and the bird went up and the shotgun swung and the bird dropped and Hank was on him and then carried the big bomber back to me. I had it mounted. A memory.

***

I put my hand palm-down out over the coals now. They are ready. Just right. The meat sizzles on the hot grill and a flame gutters up out of the drippings, then dies and the scent of cooking rises into the evening. Alder smoke.

We hunted for two days, Duane and I. Took limits home. Two daily, two in possession. The end was coming, the bag limits adjusted accordingly.

The spring after that hunt, Duane walked into his west pasture to spray weeds beneath those big mountains and his heart exploded. They did not find his body for several hours, and when they did, it appeared as if Duane had died walking. Mid-stride. His face had no grimace, no hand was clutched desperately to a fickle heart that decided that seventy-one years of ticking was long enough. Mid-step, and he was gone. Just. Like. That. A serenity in that kind of going, I think. His son called me and asked me about Duke, and I didn't even hesitate. He became a younger man's dog, and he fit in with my pack as if he had been born to it.

I flip the kabobs several times and test the meat with the tongs. Feels medium rare.

"I think it's ready."

And it is. Pink and slightly bloody, tasting of Montana alder and chili powder from New Mexico and Wyoming sagebrush and Western wide open. A good, strong taste. We laugh and toast and watch the sun chasing itself west.

Duke is still a younger man's dog, but an older younger man. He is an old dog now but he still zips, just not as far nor as long. Duane is gone. So are JD and Hank and Ace. Jim is into his eighth decade. Ike is slipping into his last year. The grouse called Gunnison is nearly gone, and is protected from the gun. The more prolific and widespread cousin is likely to be put on the Endangered Species List in a few years. No one hunts them much any more.

This one is my last. Shot five years ago out of a wide Wyoming sky and forgotten in a sportsman's cold storage. SG/08. Sage grouse, 2008. Perhaps a little freezer burned, but the fullest of tastes and the most memorable meat in the freezer.

Ben O. Williams
Parting Thoughts
A Life in the Uplands

I'm afraid if I had not chosen to come to Montana when I did, I would have missed out on so much: the knowledge gained in my long experience with gun dogs and bird guns, in search of a game bird that the local folks said couldn't be hunted.

I grew up on a small farm in northern Illinois, and during each upland-bird hunting season, my grandfather would spend a couple of days with us. If he came on weekdays, my mother would let me, a young second-grader, skip school so I could go hunting with him. I loved it.

Dressed in a wide-brimmed hat, a tweed coat, riding breeches and high rubber boots, my grandfather looked like he had just stepped out of an Edwardian Shooting Party. After a day of hunting, Grandfather would light his pipe and tell wonderful stories of living in England as a young chap, carrying a fine British sidelock, and rough-shooting over gundogs. Since those early days, game birds, bird guns and bird dogs have remained in the forefront of my thinking.

My first dog, a springer spaniel, was given to me. Mike was his name, but I sometimes called him "Mike the Bird Dog" in an effort to emphasize to my junior high schoolmates that I had a hunting dog of my very own. His adolescent years had been wasted in a large city with little space to run, which was a travesty for a dog of his pedigree. That changed when he came to live with me.

Mike soon showed such a remarkable talent to hunt that I amused myself trying to train him. I had no dog training experience, it just happened, and what blossomed was a wonderful, close-working relationship. We were beginners, both experimenting with the unfamiliar, and so eager to discover bird hunting. With my lack of hunting knowledge, Mike relied on his biological instincts and willingness to work in seeking out game birds. Oh, how he hunted the crop fields, the fencerows, and briar tangles adjacent the abandoned spur-line railroad tracks. I realized then that having a bird dog contributed a great deal to the joys of the hunting experience. A boy doesn't forget that sort of association.

It started in the 50s; English pointers were the predominant bird dogs south of the Mason-Dixon line. English setters were the grouse dogs of the North Country. Both were well established, and the breeds of choice for hunters in pursuit of North American upland game birds. Never having owned a pointing breed, it seemed the English Setter would best fit my needs hunting birds in Middle America. But that didn't happen.

After a four-year hitch in the U.S. Navy, and upon starting college, I got a part-time job training dogs at Oberlin Kennels. Walter Oberlin presented me with this opportunity, and what proved the gift of a lifetime—he introduced me to the Brittany, and convinced me that the establishment of Brittanys in the American uplands was here to stay. I became intensely interested in the breed.

After completing college, I moved westward to the high plains prairie, taking two female Brittanys with me. A pup from my mentor's kennel I named "Williams' Pride Michelangelo" arrived by train two years later, and became the male foundation of my bloodline.

When I first started hunting Montana, the pursuit of Hungarian partridge with pointing dogs was unheard of in a country dominated by big game hunters. Back then, Huns were considered impossible for man or dog to handle. This exotic, non-native bird posed a real challenge, and I became solely devoted in a crusade to prove they could be hunted successfully with pointing dogs. Persistence and success required more leather in shoes than it takes to build a western saddle.

For the past sixty years, my kennels have averaged between twelve and fourteen gun dogs. Most are from my "Williams' Pride Kennel" Brittany bloodlines, but I have added a few pointers and English setters along the way. I learned long ago that the best way to hunt Hungarian partridge in big, open steppe country is to put down as many dogs as I can handle. I have found that four canines work best for me, so I usually run two brace in the morning and two brace in the afternoon. By keeping a dozen or so physically strong and hard-changing bird dogs, I can hunt day after day.

Each one of us honors our "hunts" in our own way. My bird hunting has enriched my life, offering me far more than just the simple act of carrying a gun and having dogs afield. Along the way, it has taught me to follow a code of ethics: to respect the quarry, to learn their habits and habitat, and to sense how the birds make use of their environment. It has also made me aware of the vastness of the country, causing me to walk a little slower to appreciate what is around me.

I picked the high plains prairie as my place to be a bird hunter not because it offers a highly cardiovascular program that enhances a masculine image. I hunt, and I hunt here, because I am devoted to watching my canines doing what they were bred to do. I hunt for an excuse to carry a lovely piece of art in the form of a fine British double gun, and to occasionally shoot an iconic and challenging game bird, the Hungarian partridge. I hunt to surround myself in unscathed loveliness. Each one of these elements inhabits the root of my passion, and is tied directly to the reason I hunt.

That pretty much sums up my hunting philosophy.

Ben O. Williams
Author of Huns & Hun Hunting, The History, Habits, Habitat, and Techniques of Hunting A Great Game Bird. Bird Dog, The Instinctive Training Method, and More

Bruce Smithhammer
Afterword

I guess it's not surprising that this all started with discovery of a barren landscape, given that I've been drawn to them my whole life. The kind of country that seems big and empty, but to the trained eye and those willing to walk, reveals itself to be fecund and full of oft-overlooked detail.

In this case, that landscape was literary, and largely devoid of the experience as we knew it—mainly, DIY upland hunting on public lands.

While writing about upland hunting has a long history, much of it in the recent past seems to have devolved into formulaic "how-tos," accounts of guided trips or frankly, just unimaginative and overly sappy writing. Too often all of the above. In my mind, this left much of what made the experience so unique out of the equation. We needed more.

It's hard to accurately convey this experience without chronicling all the random, and often humorous, details that surround the actual hunt. Sometimes the drive in, or out, ends up being more adventurous than the hunt itself—the cliff-hugging mining road, scarcely wide enough for a 4x4 truck, that hopefully leads to that mesa full of chukar, leaving you puckered well after you've reached your destination. Flooring it over bentonite roads as fast as you dare with a frog-choker of a storm nipping at your heels, hoping to reach pavement before you end up stuck axles-deep for what could be days in the middle of Wyoming. Other times, it's that salty waitress giving you a rash of shit as you try to order dinner in a tiny town in Idaho, exhausted after a long hunt. With a sly wink, she knows teasing is tough love and you're the most gullible thing that has wandered through the door in a while. Or the Mennonite kid unabashedly picking his nose in a Montana cornfield as he stares at you unloading the horses. These details become such an integral part of experience, a mandatory side dish to the meat of the thing. To speak merely of shooting birds would be to do it a disservice.

I hope we have succeeded in broadening the scope of upland writing in some small way. I also hope we've succeeded in removing at least a little of the stuffing from it, and left it a little leaner, grubbier…maybe a little more honest. To Tom

Reid and Greg, and all the other contributors and readers, and of course all the (ig)noble dogs who have carried the Mouthful of Feathers spirit forward over the last decade, I sincerely thank you. We keep this dream alive by getting out there, and by never failing to be able to chuckle at the predicaments it leads to. Now put this book down, grab your dog and go get dirty.

Bruce Smithhammer *Victor, Idaho*

Meet the Authors

Michael Keaton

Michael Keaton is an acclaimed actor whose most recent work is the celebrated series, "Dopesick,." for which he won both an Emmy and a Golden Globe. He is an avid upland bird hunter and spends a great deal of time on his ranch near Big Timber, Montana.

Blaine Peetso

Blaine Peetso lives and writes in the Peace Country of Northwestern Alberta, where poetry is still a dirty word but the grouse cover is good. He is a daydreaming everyman, a discount beer connoisseur, a working-class aesthete who spends most of his time following rivers, chasing dogs and neglecting responsibilities.

Christine Peterson

Christine Peterson has written about hunting, fishing and the environment for over a decade from her home in Wyoming that she shares with her 6-year-old daughter, husband and two yellow Labradors. She writes for many publications and is a contributing writer for *Outdoor Life*. She is past president of the Outdoor Writers Association of America.

T. Edward Nickens

T. Edward Nickens has spent more than three decades reporting on conservation, field sports, and the culture of the outdoors for the world's most respected publications. He currently serves as editor-at-large for *Field & Stream*, and contributing editor for *Garden & Gun* and *Ducks Unlimited* magazines. His most recent book, *The Last Wild Road*, is a collection of essays and adventures published by Lyons Press. Nickens splits time between Raleigh and Morehead City, North Carolina, with one wife, one dog, a part-time cat, the occasional sightings of two grown children. Just don't ask him to bird hunt with you unless you mean it.

Shauna Stephenson

Shauna Stephenson lives with her husband, Tom, and two slightly feral children, Clara and Otto, at the base of the Tobacco Root Mountains in Montana. Actually, who are we kidding? They're not slightly feral, they're practically wild animals. Together they run Good Mama Farm, raise foxtrotting horses and spend summer evenings gathered around a bonfire, marveling at their blind luck to land in such an obscenely beautiful life.

Eric Thompson

Eric Thompson is a co-founder of Hardwired Outdoors LLC and an experienced bird hunter specializing in hunting the diverse and challenging game birds of the western United States. He has particular expertise in hunting pheasant, quail, grouse, and chukar, and is dedicated to pursuing these species in the rugged and remote areas of the West. With his deep knowledge of bird hunting techniques and his passion for the outdoors, Eric is a respected figure in the hunting community and is dedicated to promoting the conservation and responsible management of these important game birds.

Jillian Lukiwski

Jillian Lukiwski lives on a small working farm on the edge of the Snake River in Southern Idaho. When she isn't in her studio designing and creating jewelry as a full-time silversmith, she can be found farming garlic alongside her husband, tending her gardens, riding her horses, floating the river or following her pointing dogs through the sagebrush and canyons she calls home.

Thomas Reed

Thomas Reed is a founding member of the Mouthful of Feathers blog. He is a life-long man of the American West, the author of several books, and a long-time columnist for *Wyoming Wildlife* and *TROUT* magazines. He lives with his family on a ranch outside Pony, Montana, and helps his wife, Shauna, raise country kids, fox-trotting horses and a pack of near-wild dogs. He works for Trout Unlimited.

Bruce Smithhammer

Bruce Smithhammer is a founding member of the Mouthful of Feathers blog. He lives within spitting distance of the Tetons with his incredibly understanding Better Half. He recently had to seek counseling to help stop the chukar voices in his head. Almost everything worth knowing he has learned from dogs.

David Zoby

Dave Zoby has been publishing about the outdoors for twenty years. His essays and articles appear in *Gray's Sporting Journal*, *The Drake*, *The Sun Magazine*, and others. He lives and teaches in Casper, Wyoming.

Edgar Castillo

Edgar Castillo is a recently retired law enforcement officer for a large Kansas City metropolitan agency. He also served in the U.S. Marines. His passion lies in the uplands as he travels across the landscape or wherever the dirt road takes him; to hunt open fields, walk treelines and bust through plum thickets in search of wild birds in wild places.

Frederick Stivers

Frederick Stivers is an architectural consultant, artist and family man (an *old dad* according to his six-year-old son). Raised in the prairieland-turned-cornfields of central Illinois, he later spent a trout-fueled decade in the American West working as an architect and purveyor of "High Mountainist" style. After a spell in post-Katrina New Orleans, he returned to the Midwest to settle near St. Louis, Missouri. He typically fishes on Tuesdays if you're in the neighborhood.

Marissa Jensen

Marissa Jensen resides in Nebraska and spends her personal and professional life exploring and educating others about the beauty and importance of wild places. During the week, Jensen works as Pheasants Forever and Quail Forever's National Education & Outreach Program manager. Outside of work, she spends free time with her son and bird dogs in the uplands, on the water, or behind the lens of a camera.

Ryan Busse

Ryan Busse learned to hunt as a young boy on the high plains family ranch where he was raised. He is an author, speaker, conservation leader and amateur chef. Ryan lives with his family near Kalispell, Montana, and wishes every month was October.

Reid Bryant

Reid Bryant lives in Southern Vermont, where he works full-time for The Orvis Company, and writes around the edges of what amounts to a very fortunate life. See more of his work at www.reidbryant.com

---

Chad Love

Chad Love is a lifelong bird hunter, writer, photographer and prairie rat who lives on the high plains of western Oklahoma. Currently he works for Pheasants Forever & Quail Forever as the editor of *Quail Forever Journal*.

Chris Dombrowski

Chris Dombrowski is the author of three books of poetry and two books of nonfiction, most recently "The River You Touch". He lives in Missoula.

Els Van Woert

Els Van Woert has worked in environmental policy, conservation, sustainability, outdoor recreation and education. She recently returned to her love of creative nonfiction writing. Els adventures in the Vermont woods daily with any willing combination of her husband Simon Perkins, two children and five dogs.

Greg McReynolds

Greg McReynolds is a longtime contributor to the Mouthful of Feathers blog. He lives southeast Idaho, works for Trout Unlimited and spends his free time exploring the West with his wife, three children and a pair of English setters.

Mike Neiduski

Mike Neiduski bought a bird dog in his twenties and it changed his life. It was then he learned that most problems can be solved with a good dog out front by day and good bourbon by the fire with loved ones at night. His previous work can be found in the *Quail Forever Journal* and *Strung Magazine*.

Ben O. Williams

Ben O. Williams is an acclaimed writer, photographer, artist, and conservationist who lives in Livingston, MT. He is the author of Huns & Hun Hunting, The History, Habits, Habitat, and Techniques of Hunting A Great Game Bird, Bird Dog, The Instinctive Training Method, and many more titles.

Aknowledgements

We want to thank the writers who took the time to send us their work, the dogs who did their best even when their best did not meet human expectations, the artists for their art, and the copy editors and publishers - namely Chris Hunt and Sarah Caughie - who made it all come together. And, of course, we can't adequately thank designer James Daley for making the book look nice. We are also indebted to Frederick Stivers for his wonderful cover art.

Made in the USA
Columbia, SC
09 August 2024